The Grape

M.K. Sheikh
M.Sc. (Agri), Ph.D. (Hort)
Professor & Head
Department of Horticulture
College of Agriculture
University of Agricultural Sciences, Bijapur

Manjula N.
M.Sc. (Agri), Ph.D.
Professor & Head
Department of Agril. Extension
College of Agriculture
University of Agricultural Sciences, Bijapur

International Book Distributing Co.
(Publishing Division)

Published by
INTERNATIONAL BOOK DISTRIBUTING CO.
(Publishing Division)
Khushnuma Complex Basement
7, Meerabai Marg (Behind Jawahar Bhawan)
Lucknow 226 001 U.P. (INDIA)
Tel. : 91-522-2209542, 2209543, 2209544, 2209545
Fax : 0522-4045308
E-Mail : ibdco@airtelmail.in

First Edition 2009

Price: Rs. 650/-

ISBN 81-8189-112-0

Composed & Designed at :
Panacea Computers
3rd Floor, Agrawal Sabha Bhawan
Subhash Mohal, Sadar Cantt. Lucknow-226 002
Phone : 2483312, 9335927082, 9452295008
E-mail : prasgupt@rediffmail.com

Printed at:
Salasar Imaging Systems
C-7/5, Lawrence Road Industrial Area
Delhi - 110 035
Tel. : 011-27185653, 9810064311

भारतीय कृषि अनुसंधान संस्थान, नई दिल्ली-110012
INDIAN AGRICULTURAL RESEARCH INSTITUTE
NEW DELHI -110012 (INDIA)

डॉ० एस. ए. पाटिल
निदेशक
Dr. S. A. Patil
Director

Phones : (Off.) 2573 3367, 2584 3375
(Res.) 25733973, 25846774
Fax : +91-11-2584 6420
E-mail : director@iari.res.in

Dated: 15th May 2007

FOREWORD

Grape is an important fruit crop of India which contributes maxiumum share in the exprot of fresh fruits and vegetables. At present world production of grape is 65,486,235 MTs out of which Indian production accounts for 1.2 million tonnes of grape making a share of 1.83 per cent of world production. The area in grape has increased by 50% and its production by 71% in the country during 1994-2006. India has achieved the highest productivity of 20t/ha in the production of table grape. At present 78 per cent is used for table purpose, nearly 17-20 per cent is used for others parts of the world 80 per cent of grape is processed for making wine, raisin, juice. Except raisin the various other processed products are wine, juice, squash, syrup, jam, jelly, vinegar, pickles, chocolates, tartaric acid, oil, cattle feed, tannin etc.

The dentist feels that raisin acts as cavity fighter. Thompson seedless grape inhibit the growth of two oral bacteria *streptococcus mutans* which causes cavities and *porphyromonas gingivalis* which causes periodontal disease, and grape is also a anti-oxidant. USA is the largest producer of raisin in the world. USA and Turkery together produce 80% of the total world production. Total export of raisin is 314 mt. UK is the largest importer of raisin of about 105,500 mt, other importing countries are Germany, Russian Federation, Netherland, Canada, Japan, UAE, France, Italy Australia, Ukraine, Belgium, China and USA etc.

At persent in India grape is grown over an area of 60,000 ha with annual production of 1.6 million tonnes (FAO, 2005). About 1000 hectare in Maharashtra and 200 hectare around Bangalore in Karnataka grape wine varieties are grown around 15000 tonnes of wine grape will be ready for crushing, yield 90 lakh litres of wine annually. A wine policy in 2001 adopted by Maharashtra Grape Board, should be adopted by Karnataka Grape Board, Bangalore. The book written by Dr. M.K. Sheikh on grape will be useful to Farmers, Students, Teachers and Extension workers.

(S.A. PATIL)

Preface

Grape cultivation is one of the most lucrative farming in India. It is grown in Maharashtra, Karnatakia, Andhra Pradesh and Tamil Nadu. India produces approximately 9 lakh tonnes of tresh grape annually from an area of 34,000 ha. In the world scenario of grape experts India's share about 12,000 tonnes per year, accounting for 1.33 per cent of the total production. Grapes are grown in tropical regions of India and research goes on National Research Centre, Pune and Indian Instituure of Horticulture Research, Bangalore.

India has the distinction of grape harvesting at such a time when no grapes are harvested any where in the world by virtue of double pruning. In Northern Karnataka there is scope of cultivating wine varieties along with table varieties and resins as prices of resin decline day by day. There is immense opportunity to produce export-quality grape; off-season cropping was tried in Northern Karnataka especially Bijapur, but harvesting coincides with the September raisns.

All aspects have been covered in the booklet viz., soil, water, climate, propagation and root stock, varieties, the establishment of vineyard training, pruning systems, physiological disorders, pest and diseases, procesing and wine-making.

I sincerely hope that this book will prove useful to farmers and extension personnel in Northern Karnataka.

Dr. M.K. Sheikh

Contents

Chapter 1

Grape

In India, we are cultivating grape on an area of 1,50,000 acres and producing 12,00,000 tonnes of fruits out of which 70% are sold as table grape and from remaining 30% fruits resins are prepared.

On an average approximately around 60,000 tonnes of resins are produced in India and around 40,000 Tonnes are required for internal consumption. Looking to these figures grape cultivation looks to be not so profitable in India. Therefore, the farmers instead of producing resins they should concentrate on production of export quality grape, and little diversification is also required to cultivate wine varieties and cultivation of off-season crop. The following suggestion are needed to be adopted:

1) They should think of starting a wine park by cultivating 200 acres of grape.

2) The excise duty on wine should be removed and wine should be brought under food item on line with Mahrashtra state.

3) The National Research Centre, Pune, should come forward to spare wine variety suitable to the farming community of Bijapur area.

Grape Cultivation

In horticulture, before starting the cultivation of agri horticulture crops, their marketing knowledge and cultivation aspects are essential. The availability of land and the water with good condition suitable for irrigation and selection of rootstocks and ways to take up early crop and sustaining the crop for longer duration in more economical ways are important aspects in order to make the grape cultivation more suitable in Karnataka.

Important Points about Grape Cultivation

1) Grape, after planting, gives crop in two year's time and if goes on stock cultivation takes upto 3 years.
2) Grape is an assured crop which harvests crop till 10 years and proves to be economical.
3) When you calculate the cost of cultivation and returns, the cost-benefit ratio or the returns are good and assured.
4) Alert mind, knowledge, work in time and correct decision will lead to progress provided the farmer will help in good cultivation of grape.
5) In grape cultivation and round-the-clock-work ought to be there and the labours can be utilized all the year round.
6) Available land, water, working willingness together helps in bringing about prosperity to the grape farmers.
7) Grape cultivation is a combination of art and science, otherwise the farmers will face problem if they show negligence in any stage of crop cultivation.

Programming

1) How many acres of grape to be cultivated:

How much land you have and out of which how much is availible of good land is important. While deciding about how much area you want to bring for grape cultivation, don't select 35 guntas, 43, guntas 41 guntas etc.,

2) Where to plant grapes:

Where to take up grape cultivation for example, if you have a land in 2-3 places select only one place and for that purpose get the soil and water examined including roads, and neighbouring areas.

Farmer category	Beginning area	IInd Stage	IIIrd Stage
Economically weak	1 AC	2 AC	3 AC
Medium farmers	4 AC	8 AC	12 AC
Good farmers	10 AC	20 AC	30 AC

3) When to Plant Grape:

In Karnataka there is a practice of 'April pruning' for which the rooted cuttings are to be planted in July-August, whereas for October pruning, rooted cuttings are planted in December-January.

In Karnataka, grape fruits are available around March. If December last week or January first week is the planting time then, next year in the month of March, first crop comes for harvesting i.e., minimum of 15 month duration is required to get the first crop. That is why 4-6 months earlier planting is taken up otherwise there will be a wastage of money for maintaining upto 6 months and a loss will incure.

Grape Varieties Suitable for Cultivation:

There are several varieties of grape but considering the scope of different grape varieties decide on which are in demand in the market and which are good potential yielders. After harvesting if they are going to stand good storage life/ shelf life then or in the near future it may appear that only seedless grape may have good demand in the market. Fig. 1, 2, 3, 4 & 5.

For Example:

1) Thompson seedless 2) Sonaka

3) Kishmish charni 4) Kishmish bele

5) Ruby seedless 6) Kishmish long beli

7) Monaka
8) Centinial seedless
9) Meribian seedless
10) Black munnaka
11) Beauty seedless
12) Perlette
13) Sharad seedless
14) Flame seedless
15) Red globe
16) Clone - II

5) Maintaining distance in Grape Cultivation:

Distance between row to row should be 8 feet or 10 feet and within the row 4' and 6'. The height of the pendal should be around 6' and 6½'. After deciding the distance, the soil layers, the varieties suitable for such soil, the spraying convenience of the crop surrounding the area should be taken into account.

Digging/filling of pits:

For cultivation the following points should be born in mind. The slope of land, the north and south direction.

Type of soil	Trench depth	Trench width
Medium	45 cm	45 cm
Heavy, black soil	75 cm.	45 cm.
Murum light	45 cm	30 cm
Light soil	60 cm	60 cm

In the month of June, crops like greengram, horse gram, bean, redgram, soybean or sowing of green manure crop, viz sunhemp are advocated and in September-October after filling up the trench with good soil, the planting of rooted cuttings should be taken up in December-January. Examine the soil profile of one metre depth and get it examined for N.P.K., micro-nutrient, pH, EC, RAC etc.,

7) Rooted Cuttings:

Observe a good variety, without any disease, and get it

guaranteed also from a reputed garden as to when it is going to have fruits. While bringing the canes confirm that it should have an age of 5-6 years and after bringing the canes 2-3 cutting should be made from each cane. Decide the rooted cutting you want in that case; you should take double the quantity and treat them with fungicide, IBA-1000 ppm, then plant it in the bed or packets applying FYM and DAP. Afterwards, spray

Filling of Trench with the following Material

Sl. No.	Quantity of fertilizer/Ac	Medium soil	Heavy soil	Light soil
1	Green manure (sunhemp)	One acre	2½Acre	1½Acre
2	Compost	3 Truck load	4Truck load	5 Truck load
3	7.10.5 (Sterameal)	750 kg	750 kg	750 kg
4	DAP	100 kg	100 kg	150 kg
5	SOP	100 kg	100 kg	100 kg
6	Single superphosphate	100 kg	100 kg	100 kg
7	Neem cake	750 kg	750 kg	750 kg
8	Magnesium sulphate	25 kg	20 kg	30 kg
9	Calcium: magnesium	50 kg	100 kg	100 kg
10	Ferrous sulphate	5 kg	15 kg	10 kg
11	Zinc sulphate	5 kg	15 kg	12 kg
12	Borax	1 kg	2 kg	5 kg
13	Mixture of micro-organism	15 kg	30 kg	30 kg
14	Vermicompost	20 kg	15 kg	15 kg
15	Organic fertilizer	100 kg	500 kg	500 kg

BM-1%, two to three times and mix DAP 1 kg plus magnesium sulphate ½ kg in 100 liters and spray. The cuttings will be ready for planting in a couple of months time.

Use of root stocks in grape:

Root stock means what:

1) In Santara, Mosambi-Jamberi Rangpur rootstocks are used.

2) Sapota is grafted on Khirni, Rayan Therefore, Grape on grape should be grafted and used with justifying background of root stocks requiring;

1) To take maximum yield/acre.

2) To increase grape quality,

3) To reduce cost of grape cultivation,

4) To overcome more akalinity/sodicity problem.

At present grape is cultivated by planting the rooted cuttings, from April & October pruning. Now grape area is expanding and people want to take up grape cultivation in problematic soils by using root stocks which can overcome the problems of high EC, high sodicity, akalinity, high pH etc.

Nowadays, our grape export is increasing and from 2004 free trade has begun.

Characteristics of root stocks:

1) Resistance to phylloxera;

2) Resistance to salt;

3) Increase in yield;

4) Resistance to drought;

Types of root stocks:

Dogridge, Ramsay, Salt Creek, 1619, 1616, 1613, SO_4 Champion, 49B, 1103P. Fig-6.1, 6.2, 6.3

Insitu Grafting:

1) First planting of rootstocks in the month of January-February viz. Dogridge, 1619, Ramsay (anyone)
2) Wedge grafting in the month of September-October.
3) Selecting two good branches of root stocks that can be utilized for making cuttings of root stocks.

There are two methods of grafting:

1) Insitu grafting;
2) Preparation of rooted cutting to go for wedge grafting and after 3 months of hardening the grafted plants are ready for sale/planting.

Layout of garden:

The planting distance needs to be decided by the farmer, after which he has to mark the points by using a rope. Dig the Trenches thereafter, so that planting is taken up by selecting disease and insect-free planting material. Drench with bordeux mixture (1%) and press the soil around the plant.

Care after Planting:

1) During November-December after planting, keep an eye on the plant by observing whether proper irrigation is going on or not. The plant should grow uniformly in November but as cold temperature exists, the growth

Time/ month	Nutrition	After Care	Watering	Other
October	During planting time apply starter solutions.	After and before planting apply BM 1 %	After planting one light irrigation	Full plant
November 1-10	Foliar spray of Mahagreen	BM 1% spray insecticide + wet sulphur spray	one irrigation.	

Time/ month	Nutrition	After Care	Watering	Other
11-20	Ammonium Sulphate-50 kg $Mg.SO_4$, 10 kg to soil/AC.	Foliar spray of insecticide	one-irrigation	
November 21-30	Ammonium Sulphate 75 kg	Wet. Sulf. spray. one irrigation		
December 1-10	$MgSo_4$ 12 kg/AC	BHC -10% 5kg plus 300 mesh Wet. sulf. Powder.		-
Dec 11-20	DAP-50 kg 7:10:5-100 kg Neemcake-200 kg	Fungicide + insecticide spray	irrigation	-
December 21-31	Magnesium Sulphate spray 0.2%	-	Irrigation	-

might not be fast. The phosphate might not be fully available. Taking all the points into consideration, decision has to be taken.

Aftercare of new plantation:

Give support to the plants with the help of bamboo and encourage proper and uniform growth, take bottom cut, keep 3 buds at the bottom when they sprout. By February work should be completed. Before the rains, keep the garden clean,

Time/ month	Work to be attended	Crop Care	Nutrition	Irrigation
January 1-10	Bottom cut, bamboo support	BM 1% drenching	-	irrigation

Time/ month	Work to be attended	Crop Care	Nutrition	Irrigation
Jan -11-20	Tying of vine to bamboo support	spraying of insecticide	-	one irrigation
Jan 21-30	Tying of vine and erecting of pendal	Fungicide spraying	-	one irrigation
Feb 1-10	-do-	Insecticide + fungicide spraying	-	one irrigation
Feb 11-20	-do-	Lihocin 500 ppm spraying.	DAP 50 kg or 7:10:5 100 kg Neem cake 250 kg	one irrigation
Feb 21-28	-	-	Bone meal 100 kg	one irrigation

encourage two T and each T should have 12-14 canes and each cane should be nipped at 15 leaves.

Month/ Time	Work to be attended	Crop Care	Nutri-tion	Irrigation
March 1-15	Encouraging main arm or T on both sides	Fungicide and insecticide spraying of BM-0.5%	-	2 irrigation
March 1-15	Nipping on T tip at 8th leaf	BM spraying 0.5%	Lihocin of 500 ppm	2 irrigation

Month/ Time	Work to be attended	Crop Care	Nutrition	Irrigation
April - 1-15	Keeping 5-7 canes on each T	DAP 1 kg + $MgSO_4$ - ½kg/100 lit spraying	-	2 irrigation
April - 16-30	Above work to be completed	BM spraying 0.5 % FYM -1 truck 7:10:5 100 kg Neem cake-100kg	-	2 irrigation
May 1-15	-	200 kg bio-fertilizer	-	3 irrigation
May - 16-15	-	BM-0.5%	-	3 irrigation

By February end, the sprouting will be there and by keeping 5-6 leaves the auxiliary growth should be removed.

June to September:

1) Before the rain starts, the number of canes should be encouraged properly.
2) Wherever the cane is kept, its excess growth should be stopped.
3) Nip the canes at the 15th leaf.
4) Double plants removed from the garden.
5) Keep the pest and disease in control.
6) Excess canes to be removed.
7) Encourage green manure cultivation.

To implement the above points, the future course of action will be as follows:

June;

1) Maintaining the canes i.e., for one square feet area and one cane should be retained and excess canes be removed immediately.
2) Stop growth of each cane at 15th leaf.
3) The canes usually possess excess and unwanted growth in the leaf axil, which should be removed. i.e., 2-3 leaf.
4) Take up spraying of lihocin @ 500 ppm.
5) Take up foliar spraying of bordeux mixture (0.5%).

July;

1) Examine the condition of canes if they are not good, restrict them to 10%.
2) To enrich the canes give micro-nutrient spray.
3) Don't allow excess rainwater to stand in the field.

August;

If excess growth is observed then curb it and whatever the necessary steps required implement during September and October. Prepare to carry out necessary things such as, labour, dormex application, secatures which should be dipped in formalin to disinfect, observe to dieback and stem borer etc.,

Erection of Pendal;

The erection of pendal is necessary because it gives support to the plant/vine, helps the vine spread properly, helps in pruning. Then spread the canes on wires, facilitate easy application of fertilizer, spray insecticide and fungicide. Harvest sunlight etc. It helps to save cost of cultivation.

Types of training system;

There are several types of training system:

1) Pendal or bower system

2) Four-arm kniffin system
3) Y-Trellis
4) Telephone system
5) Extended Australian gable system.

Every system has got its own advantages and disadvantages. Lot of researches have been conducted on different training system, of which T and Y system are most ideal to the present situation. Fig-7, 8, 9 & 10.

The Advantages of T and Y system:

1) The system will be tough and long-lasting.
2) Care of every cane is possible.
3) Exposure to direct sunlight can be avoided.
4) Spraying of insecticide, fungicide and harmon will be easy.
5) Drip irrigation system is most suitable.
6) Increases the grape bunch quality.
7) Per acre production of grape will be enhanced.

Requirement of one acre 'T' training system:

Area-1 Acre, or 0.4 hectare, 43560 cm square ft i.e, 212 x 205 = 43560 + 100 sq. ft, tank, filter fixing area, cultivable area = 200 feet long x 200 width.

= 40, 000 sq. ft.

Details of requirement of steel for 'T' system:

Types	Number	Size cm x mm	Per Acre 200 Lines	
			Number	Total
Corner stone poles	2	8 x 2.5 x 2	40	320
Supporting poles	2	8 x 2.5 x 2	40	320

Types	Number	Size cm x mm	Per Acre 200 Lines	
			Number	Total
Inside poles	7	8 x 2.5 x 2	140	1120
T	9	4 x 2.5 x 2	180	720
T support	18	2 x 2.5 x 2	360	720
Hole pass bar	22	1 x 1 x 0	440	440

One line requirement **One acre requirement**

	Holes	Nut & Bolt	1 Bolts	Holes	Nut & Bolt	1 Bolts
Inners	7 x 10	7 x 3	-	1400	420	-
Outers	2 x 10	2 x 3	2 x 10	400	120	400
Support	2 x 3	1 x 2	-	120	40	-
Total				1920	580	400
				2000	600	400

Leave 10 feet space in the east and west sides and 25 feet for north south.

16 long steel (20 + 20 + 70 + 90 = 200 Nos of pieces)

Iron bar - 20 feet long = 22 in Nos.

GI bar - 12 gauge

<u>One line (running foot)</u> <u>One acre requirement</u>

200 x 5 = 1000 ft. = 20000 ft.

Cutting works = Poles 16 ft. long for every two units in two 220 = 440 pieces.

16 feet for every 4 unit x 180 and from 8 Nos.

360 Numbers have to be made.

Steel bar 5 feet, 440 in number, with a total of 2200.

Wires 200 ft. and, 100 pieces.

For erection of 'T' pendal and of fix up the poles

For every line	For every acre
2 x 2 2.5 x 11 pits	11 x 20 = 220 pits
11 x 10 = 110 Ghan foot	2200 Ghan ft.

Details of concrete requirement (for one acre)

1) Sand = sieved = 4 brass
2) Khadi = ½" = 3 brass
3) Khadi = ¼" = 3 brass
4) Dambar or coal tar = 2 brass
5) Cement = - 40 bags.

After completion of concrete work, wire work needs to be taken up and to all steel poles apply oil paint or red oxide.

Bamboo support

To each vine, bamboo support is necessary. About 1000 bamboos are required. Bottom of the bamboo should be applied with coaltar and on top apply oil paint or red oxide.

Details of pendal erection:

1) Steel pole, approximately 2 tonnes
2) G.I. wire, approximately 1.5 tonnes
3) Pass bars, approximately 0.4 tonnes
4) Nut and bolt, approximately 0.4 tonnes
5) I bolt, approximately 0.2 tonne

Expenditure on erection of pendal:	**Rupees**
1) Sand and transport=	1000-00
2) Khadi and transport =	1000-00
3) Dambar =	500-00
4) Cement =	6500-00
5) Painting cutting/fitting/Erecting =	6000-00
6) 1000 bamboos Nos. =	5000-00
7) Painting, fixing in pits and tying =	2500-00
	Total Rs. 16,000-00

Chapter 2

Varities of Grape

1. Anab-e-shahi

Trunk large, to very large, cane large and thick, dark brown. Leaves cordate moderally pubescent, emerging leaves light green with pink tinge, inflorescence fairly compact bunch very large, slightly shoulderd or conical, uniform ripening, medium to high shattering.

2. Bangalore Blue

It is a vinifera and labrusca hybrid vines vigrous, bark very loose, canes brown long, thick, tendril greyish green mostly bi-fid, some time tri fid. Fully grown leaves tri lobed to 5 lobed. Ripening fairly uniform in South.

3. Thompson Seedless

Berry are elongish it ripens uniformly it does well on Kniffin system, telephone system, it is succeptible to downy disease flower hermophrodite.

4. Arkavati

A hybrid, crossed between Black champa x Thompson seedless, vines vigrous, cluster medium size, well filled long conical to cylindrical, berries medium. Tss 25%

5. Arka Hans:

A cross between Bangalore blue x Anab-e-Shahi are moderatly vigrous cluster medium size, Tss-18-21%. It is suitable to head system.

6. Arka Kanchan

A cross between Anab-e-Shahi x Queen of vine yard

medium to large. Tss - 19-22%. It is late ripening with poor keeping quality.

7. Arka Shym

A cross between Bangalore blue x Black champa vines are moderatly vigrous, cluster medium size, berries medium size. Yield potential very good. It is very good for dry red table wine.

8. Maroo seedless, superior seedless, Flame seedless, Red globe are newly introduced.

9. Among the wine varities shiraz, Merlotte, Cabernet savignon, Zinfenda, Pinot Noir are promising.

10. Sonaka

A mutant of Thompson seedless, bunch medium to large, berries long, fetch good price in market.

11. Sharad Seedless

A black varitey, medium size bunch. Alternate bearing is observed. More preferred at Christmass festival.

12. Flame Seedless:

Uneven ripening is a problem, otherwise a good variety.

13. Redglobe:

It is getting premium price in market.

14. Fantacy

It is also a very good variety in grape, medium size bunch.

15. Tas-A-Ganesh

A mutant of Thompson Seedless

16. Clone II

A mutant of Thompson Seedless yield 10% more than Thompson Seedless.

Chapter 3

Scope for Grape Industry in India for Export

Present status of grape growing in the country:

As per the data and information available, it is estimated that the total area under grape cultivation in the country is about 50,000 hectare with annual production of about 10-12 lakh metric tonnes of fresh grape.

Distribution of Area

1) Karnataka:

Karnataka is the second largest state in the country having about 10,000 hectares under grape. Bangalore, Bagalkot, Kolar and Bijapur are the main grape growing districts.

Varieties:

Bangalore purple, Bangalore blue. Thompson seedless are the main varieties under cultivation. Other varieties like Arakavati, Neelmani, Flame seedless, Sharad Seedless, Sonaka, Clone-II, Red globe are now becoming popular among the growers.

2) Maharashtra:

Nasik, Sangli, Solapur, Pune, Osmanabad are the major grape growing districts of Mahrasthra having about 16,000 hectares with annual production of about 3 lakh metric tonnes per year

Major Varieties Under Cultivation-

Thompson seedless, Tas-e Ganesh, Sonaka are the main

varieties. Manik Chaman, Kishmish Charani, Sharad Seedless, Flame Seedless are also getting popular. All these varieties are seedless and their total share is more than 80% in the acrege and production.

3) Andhra Pradesh:

Hyderabad is well known for grape cultivation since a long time and the cultivation has remained concentrated in about 75 km. radius of the twin city of Secundrabad and Hyderabad. The total area is about 6,000 hectare and the main variety grown is Anab-e-Shahi. In recent years, Dilkush, Flame seedless, Thompson Seedless and Sonaka are getting increasing demand among the growers and consumers.

4) Grape growing in North:

Punjab, Haryana, and Himachal Pradesh are known for grape cultivation. However the expansion was not boosted mainly due to climatic conditious. Anab-e-Shahi and Perlette etc. are the varieties grown here. Total area in these states together do not exceed beyound 10,000 hectares.

Importance and Scope for Export:

Starting from 1985 the country is exporting in an increasing and highly dignified manner specially after 1990. The export is done mainly to the middle eastern countries and european market. Also new markets viz. Hongkong, Singapore and Japan are showing much interest.

Pomegranate, mango, are the major fruit crops having economic importance. But as compared to others, grape is enjoying a special privilege in exports. Apart from fresh table grape other products of grapes like raisin, juice and wine products also have export potential.

Policies of Central and State Governments' Foreign collaboration, growers union, cooperative sector, state agricultural universities, innovative growers and scientist, extension workers together are joining hands with research and development organizations. The National Research Centre, the APEDA, the Karnataka State Marketing Board have a very potential role to play in export.

Putting all efforts together we have a scope to export one lakh tonnes of fresh table grapes every year in the near future.

Planning and Production:

Instead of collecting selected crops from diversified vine yards for export we should select vine yards for export of grapes.

This can be done by planning in advance. There should be a set of growers in different agro-climatic situations with each having 40 ha vine yard from where 800-1000 tonnes of grape of export quality could be produced. These areas should be managed with similar package of practices for one variety.

Converting the present plantation on this line and bringing new area under this programme a planning is required. It should be remembered that this cultivation is exclusively for export purposes.

After acheiving the target the post-harvest treatment and other infrastructure should also be developed simultaneously. The planning should be framed with proper execution and supervision. the production and procurement should be frequently monitered by a committee on a scientific level and commercial with a strong administrative back-up.

Work should be simultaneously done in Karnataka, Maharashtra, Andhra Pradesh, Tamil Nadu with each having a regional sub-committee with financial support. It should have its headquarter at Bangalore with the support of National Grape Federation of India.

Grape Export

1) Grape production in Karnataka is quality-wise good.
2) Good production and quality leads to more demand for

grape in the country and also outside for exports.

3) However as long as we send the grape, its rate increases.

4) By Exporting grape the farmers get good returns specially foreign exchange or dollars.

5) European and Middle East countries' demand is increasing day-by-day.

6) The countries which are nearer to us are Japan, Hong kong, and The Philippines which are importing grape from us.

Export of Grape in a wide network

The grape which is produced in India has trade links with Bangladesh, Pakistan, Nepal, Myanmar and Sri Lanka.

Among these countries Sri Lanka requires sea route whereas others by road/railways. Apart from these neighbouring countries, other European countries are our customers, besides Saudi Arabia, Iran, Iraq, Kuwait, Syria, and European countries viz, England, France, Italy, Spain, Germany etc.

The countries which have less demand are Bangladesh, Nepal and Sri Lanka.

Medium Demand: Saudi Arabia, Iran, Iraq and Kuwait

More Demand: England, France, Italy and Germany.

While exporting grape there are several points one has to keep in mind and they are:

1) **Monetarily strong ones** : The countries to which we are exporting their financial condition should be good which means demand will also be good. In Middle Eastern countries, there are petroleum products which mean good whereas in European countries, there is good purchasing power due to their sound economy.

   If the population of a country is enormous then the purchasing power will be less. And that is to be borne in mind.

2) **Necessity** means food, clothing and shelter. If that is there then the luxury items like grape they can afford to get.

3) The demand for our grape in some of the countries has be to studied first, then only go for export and find how the demand is existing and list down the countries which require our grape.

European Countries Grape Demand:

Among the European countries demand from England for our grape is good because from April-June onwards nowhere in the world grape is available except India. Since last 10-15 years in England the market study showed that our market was having encouraging trend from last 5-7 years. The grape consumption rose from 70 to one lakh tonnes and every year the consumption trends increased. About 88% of demand is fulfilled, from countries viz., Spain (25%) Italy (25%) South Africa (13%), Greece (11%) Cyprus (7%) Chili (7%) which are supplying to the super market during December to June. France also imports grape at the same time when England imports.

From Spain, South Africa and Chile the grape is exported to Netherlands and Belgium which are main exporters to Italy, South Africa and Chile. So it appears that European market is a big market for grape. European people consume lot of fresh grape because of their good purchasing power.

Sl. No.	Exporting countries	Yearly export	Where they export
1	South Africa	45.5 thousand tones	Germany, England, (75%-80%)
2	Chile	3000 tonnes	America, Netherlands, England (70-75%)
3	Australia	12-1500 tonnes	England (50-60%)

It appears that from South Africa, Chile, Australia grape is being exported to England. So one has to understand the Government rules and regulation and what precautionary measures one has to take and which variety they prefer. One has to consider all these information not only for today but also for the future. Among the European countries, England's demand is fulfilled by Chile, South Africa and Australia, grape is available form January and from those countries England have captured big departmental stores. In India we are producing export quality grape at par with other departmental stores in England.

Today in India the availability of grape starts from January and continues upto May with peak availability in the month of March. So we can export grape from January to March in large quantity. From April to June the demand for grape will be reduced. In India we are growing several varieties. To establish a variety in a particular region it will take many years to test its suitability. For example from Australia there is a variety called, Mermen seedless, from Afghanistan, Kishmish long beli and from California centenial seedless. For all these a separate package of practice is required from IIHR, Bangalore. Arkavati seedless and few year back Kishmish Beli and Kishmish Charanai were brought to India from Russia and there testing is going on. Kishmish beli as compared to Thompson seedless comes to harvest early in January and it is available in the market and it will suit our climatic situation in India. Early availability of grape is possible by modification of pruning in time. At present we are taking up pruning in October and early pruning has to be planned in August so that by December the grape will be ready for harvest.

If October pruning is done in August then we are going to face some problems like incidence of disease but we can control it. However, the advantageous thing is that we can harvest them by January to March which facilitates exports into the European markets. In Karnataka temperature, rainfall and humidity are the three important factor for grape cultivation which are most suitable and here seedless grape is being cultivated very well and is heading time to market in January for consumption.

Quality Consideration

It is the quality and not the quantity that is important for exports. Everything about quality should be taught to the growers who are cultivating grape for export purposes. The requirement from various markets will have to be surveyed and considering the local situations, including climate and soil, pocketwise recommendation of qualitative analysis ought to be laid out on the following points:

1) Variety 2) season 3) productivity 4) optimum yield (5) bunch size/shape (6) appearance and weight (7) berry size, shape and colour (8) Tss, acidity, and specific gravity (9) taste, Flavour and appearance (10) adherence and chemical residue. These can be further elaborated considering the present knowledge and experience:

1) Variety: Thompson seedless and Tas-e-Ganesh some more introductions should also be considered.
2) Bunch shape: oblong/conical
3) Bunch weight: 400-600 gm.
4) Berry; spherical: greenish, diameter above 18 mm weight 3 to 5gm.
5) firmness: Firm, strong, and pulpy.
6) Tss: 18° to 22° brix, acidity-0.5 to 0.65.
7) No spot-bruises, no chemical residue.
8) No taste and other oddities.
9) There should be standard relations in (1) yield/ha (2) quality and (3) cost of production.

Production and Quality:

In Karnataka seedless grape, on an average the farmers are producing around 20 tonnes to 25 tonnes per hectare. There is lot of controversy regarding quality as less production coincides with good quality. Similarly more production tallies with poor quality grape. But for export if a farmer is producing 25-30 tonnes per hectare, it will not be possible to produce quality fruits. For producing quality fruits for export one has to keep the following points in mind:

1) **Grape Variety**: _We are growing about 4-5 seedless grape varieties, out of which Tas-e Ganesh and Thompson seedless, being the varieties that are having very good shape and good shelf life specially the berries that are longish. The leaves of these varieties are thick. They stay perserved for a long time, hence helps in getting good crop.

2) **Yield:** In our place the yield starts from the second year onwards and continues till 15 years, thereafter when it becomes old the yield declines. After 6-7 years the setting will change depending upon the nutrition practice. The garden in which vines are of 3 to 7 years, will produce export quality grapes.

   To build such vigour the vines have to be rejuvenated.

3) **Requirement of soil and water:** for good quality grape production, the soil and water quality should be good. In our place many of our grape gardens are having lime nodules in the bottom and high pH and EC. Under such situation utmost care is required. If the soil contains 10 per cent lime avoid cultivation of grape. The water which is free from chlorine and sodium should be utilized. Coincidence of good soil with bad water and bad soil makes the situation difficult for high quality grape cultivation leading to higher cost of cultivation with less returns. In such gardens where export quality production

is possible the farmers are requested to go for testing of water and soil to have proper balanced application of fertilizer for availability of NPK and micro-nutrients. These three points are fundamental and only based on these the improvement is possible.

The details of how to produce good quality grape will be discussed in the next chapters. Second important point to be considered is, if your garden age is more than 7-8 years then rejuvenate such gardens by going for thinning. If the main stem are affected by stem borer or dieback, such vines are also cut at the bottom to rejuvenate in a new plant or if you want to convert the variety into another, e.g., Thompson seedless, then it can be grafted.

Third point is that when the soil is not problematic then usually water as a rule also will not be problematic. The soil and water character will not change immediately but it takes many years to see the difference. But in case of get change then the problem starts. If the pH of the soil is high then to get a good grape crop is very difficult and it requires high expenditure under such circumstances, requireing application of green manure and bio-fertilizers.

The above three points are very important that one has to keep in mind.

Chapter 4

Training System in Grape

Good number of training system are in practice in India like Bower system, Kniffin system, Telephone System, Head system, Y-Trellis System (California System), GDC Geneva double curtain system.

1. Bower system

This system is suitable to all varities. The spacing followed is 6' x 4' which accomdate 1800 plants per acre and yielding about 15 to 18 tonnes/Ac, but apical dominance is more predominant the cost benefit ratio is also more.

2. Kniffin System

This is also called Espalier system. It help in developing vertical canopy. This system is expensive than Bower system Disease incidence is less as compared to Bower System.

3. Telephone System

T-trellis is used in this system,it is a mini-discontinous bower system with three top wires and T shaped support the trellis look like telephone system.

This system in suitable to moderatly vigrous variety. Yield less than bower system. In hot and dry places, sun burn of berries, arms in summer is notices.

4. Head System

Cost benefit ratio is least, also called umbrella system, around 4500 plants can be accomodated per hectare. The vines are supported to vertical stakes.

5. Geneva double curtain

This is improvement over single codon system using a T-trellis.

6. Y-System

This is a divided and open canopy system. The angle between two arms of Y can be 100 to 110°, while the length of the cross arm is 90-120 cm.

Double pruning

This system is followed in Northern Karnataka in Thompson seedless. As soon as the harvest over by Summer, the vines are subjected to rest for a month, during which water is with held for storage. All the canes are pruned back to spur, retaining on one basal node, this is called April pruning or back pruning or foundation pruning, summer pruning, buds get differentiated to flower primordia and shoots matures in 150 days, these mature shoots are pruned for fruiting before the winter season called fore pruning or September October pruning, depending on long cane, sub-cane pruning is done in Thompson seedless sevent bud is most potential.

Chapter 5

Need of Root stock in Grape

Grape is grown on an area of 45000 hectare with an annual production of 1,20,000 Tonnes in Maharashtra and in Karnataka it is grown on an area of 12000 hectare with a production of 1,65,000 tonnes. With reports of declining yield is the states viz Maharashtra and Northern Karnataka due to salinily of soil and water and severe drought the farmers have realised the importance of root stock. In California the root stocks are used against phylloxera a root aphid, salt resistants and drought resistant, and the root stocks are the answer for this problem. Grape vine when grown on their own root, production of export quality grape becasue a difficult task and when they grown on root stock looking to the soil and water reprots, different root stock are available and they can be utilized for different situation. The soil are alkaline saline.

In Northern Karnataka chloride content in irrigation water is a major problem because of excess level of sodium and calcium which are freely available root stock species vitis champini can grow very well because it is deep rooted and it can absorbs the filter water from deeper zone. The root stock can be propagated by seeds, cuttings, layers and to get the 100 per cent purily they can also be clonaly propagated. The grafting on these root stock is easy by wedge grafting by planting the root stock in January - February and grafting in October same year. To over come the problem of salinity the Horticulture practices like salt leaching amendment of soil, application of sawdust, opening of trenches to leach out the soluble salts like sodium etc. green manuring like growing of sunhemp, and incorporating in soil when it flowers, mulching with straw, plastic etc also help to overcome these problems, but the results were not encouraging. Hence growing of root stocks like Dog ridge (All situation) 1103 R (Drought tolerant), 99 Ritcher (Drought tolerant) 110 Ritcher (Drought tolerant) So4 (1 lime tolerant) Ramsey (tolerant to saline soil) St. George (Drought tolerent) The root stocks which are Drought resistant and good to solve the problem of salinity because they are having effective mechanism of ion from the soil, as they will not absorb the CI and Na^+ and take up only beneficial ions which are not harmful to plants.

Why to use root stock:

Try to find out the problem of grape cultivation because the ideal soil is the one where pH less than 8.5, EC less than 2-2.5 mm hos/cm^2. Exchangeable sodium percentage less than 15 and free calcium 10-12 per cent. The water for grape cultivation the Electric conductivity should be less than 1 mm hos/cm^2, SAR less than 8, meq/liter, all the above soil situations are difficult to available. If the above said situation of soil and water are available then there is no need to employ the root stock otherwise which leads to fast growth, more production of leaf, naturally the cost of cultivation may go up and to suppress the growth use of CCC may cost more because it is ant gibberlin. Root stock also help in nutrient uptake but zinc deficiency is more predominant. By cultivation on root stock the qulaity and productivity will also be more. Under saline soil situation if EC > 4 mm hose, ESP <15, pH < 8.5 Ec is directly related to chlarine which causes leaf margin burning, leaf becomes rubbery when crumbled in hand palm, the plant show stunted growth, pre-mature leaf drop, Internodal lenght is reduced, less yield Dogridge, 110R, 1103P. Salt Greek are good in over coming the problem of salinity, with Bangalore. Dogridge root stock the conc. of soluble salts EC 3.8 dsm-1, safe limit of clorine is 3 mequivalent (me) per liter and with root stock upto 18 meq/litre. In sodic soils whch is a problem in sub-tropical regions. The soils are said to be alkaline when the EC of saturation extract is less than 2 ds/m, ESP > 15%, pH 8-10, the growth under such situation will be affected with slender shoot, smaller size leaves, short internodal length and such soils are not fit for cultivation.

In sub-Tropical regions the demand for water will be more as the maximum evapo-transpirzation loss in Northern Karnataka is 9-10 mm/ day, specially at Bijapur, the water is available at a very deeper level, they go for rigging upto 650 feet, the quality of water is poor because less per colation, the rain water go as run off & forms gulleys but do not go in to the soil because these region soil are Black soil or clay soil where the potash content is high (KCl) and water per colation is very less and the problem get aggrevated in summer or whereever drought situation are observed not necessary in summer only but other part of the year also, under such situation the berry size get reduced, less number of canes, sun burn of grape bunches, which further leads to reduction in qualtiy for export because the export qualtiy bunch should be milky green.

As the root stock roots go very deep & away from stem, hence water and nutrient availabity of nutrient also will be good and it can also be minimized. Dogridged root stock is an efficient user of availble potassium and available nitrate. Root stocks have an important role to change the shoot vigour and bring equlibrium in vegetative and productive growth, quality and yield, they also help in fruit bud differentiation & they are also capable of Cytokinin synthesization in their toots. 1613 root stock also synthesieze more cytokinin than own root Thompson seedless roots, high cytokenin. Giberllin is known for good fruit bud differentiation, becuase more bud break more yield, when Thompson seedless was grafted on 1613 root stock the yield were more in farmers field.

Research conducted in India and other parts of the world have identified that root stock are resistant to salinity, alkinity, drought, root stock helps in increased fruit bud differentiation resulting in more productivity.

The root stock 1103 R, 140 R, 110 R, 450 A, 99R St. George are suitable to drought situation or water shortage problem, the root stock like Dogridge, 140 U, 99R. 110 R, Ramsey are suitable to the situation of soil EC>2 mm hos/cm^2, water EC > mm hos/cm^2, the root stocks Dogridge, 1613, Ramsey to a situation of soil ESp more than, 15 or water SAR > 8, the root stock Fercal, SO4, 420 A are suitable where free content of the water is > 4 meq/ litre than the root stocks viz. Dogridge, Ramsey Teleki for increased Nitrogen potassium content Dogridge is suitable. The Morphological character of Dogridge viz leaf shape is cordate (Heart shape) petiole colour purplish.

Propagation of root stock is mostly done by hard wood cuttings they should be of last season growth. The plant you select should grow vigrously and free from any disease viz Viral, Bacterial, Fungal.

The cuttings should be medium in size with optimum internodal length they should not be flat or angular when you observe the section, the cutting should be selected from the middle portion and preferablyof 6-9 inches in length with 4-5 buds, the cuttings should be soaked in water for 24 hours then in IBA solution with a conc. of 2000 to 2600 ppm for 5-10 seconds helps in better rooting or some time applicaiton of *Trichoderma herzianum,* also helps in rooting. The poly bags should have a size of 9" x 6" with 200 -250 gauge thickness, the planting media is good Red soil with vermicompost : sand : Farm Yard Manure in 1:1:1:1 proportion and insert two buds into the packet and 2 to 3 buds above the media. The packet should have holes at sides and at bottom and apply few granules of phorate or Furadon, or Carbofuron etc. to over come the problem of Termite attack or apply chloropyriphos 4ml/liter of water.

There is also a practice of grafting by machine where selected scion and root stock pieces get interlocked by pressing the machine, they are dipped in liquid paraffine, then they are kept in controlled atmosphere chamber where relative humidity and temperature are controlled, in few days scion and root stock sprouts without any soil media such plants are available at Rs. 20-30/each some time Ramsey root stock which is most suitable to wine varities like Shiraz pinot Noir, Merlot, Zinfendal, Cabernet Savignon are available at Narayan gaon Nasik.

Some time after opening the treches and application of super phosphate 500 gm per running meter, FYM micronutrient, Green manure/5 kg per plant, 2-3 cuttings of Thompson seedless or desired variety can be planted directly after treatment with IBA solution having a conc. of 2000-2500 ppm after sprouting of the cutting the vigrous one will be retained and grafting is done during October. Extra care should be taken against the termite attack by application with Neem cake/ Chlorophyriphos 4 ml/liter of water every 15 days once. For control of powdery mildew spray carbendenzim 1 gm./ litre of water, Anthracnose spray Thiophenate methyl 1 gm/ lit, Downy mildew 2 gm (metalexil + Mancozeb) / litre of water. Some time mist chambers are utilized for proper rootings in grape cuttings. The grape cuttings can be selected from the Sept. -October pruning because the tempreture and humidity will be suitable for sprouting rootings the cuttings also get 3-4 months time to develop till the planting starts by February.

Some time the beds are prepared having a size of 5' x 2' x 6" a good red soil, FYM are applied after treating with IBA 2000 to 2600 ppm for 5 seconds, they are planted. But cuttings should be planted in polythene bags only for long distance transport.

The farmers can also construct the zero energy chambers at their field. They are double wall tanks with15-20 cm gap between two walls, the inner diameter of the tank should be 180 cm in width, 150 cm in height, and 600 cm in length outside wall should have a length of 650 cm, height 150 cm and width 230 cm, sand is filled inside the inner tank upto a height of 50 cm, the sand is filled in between two walls and soaked till it reaches saturation or a dripper is installed in between the two walls. Half matured cuttings are selected with 4-5 nodes the cuttings are dipped in 1100 ppm IBA for 60 seconds and planted in sand, the tank is covered with 750 guage covers. It takes about one month to start rooting then rooted cuttings are transferred to poly bags filled with vermicompost, sand, FYM, Red soil in 1:1:1:1 proportion and kept out side to sustain the out side heat.

Once the cuttings attains the age of 6 months they are transplanted in the field for establishment. The land should be prepared by levelling with tractor, the weeds like *Cynadon dactylon* and *Cyprus rotundus* should be completely controlled by application of Glyphosate @ 5-6 ml/lit for Cyanadon and 10-12 ml/lit. for *Cyprus rotundus* or manual labours can be engaged. some time two to three sprays may also be used to control the weeds other wise they compete for nutrient and water, if there is a water shortage problem, then diffuser can also be used which minimises the water requirement of the crop. A 2' x 2'½ trench with convinient length is opened preferrably in south-north direction and keep the top soil at one side, after sufficient exposure to sunlight the top soil is filled or some time if it is murum soil then red soil should be filled grape is also cultivated in Medium black size in Belgaum Distt. in Karnataka with good drainage system with 1' width x 2-2½' deep Trench. So that the water table is brought down, then the root stocks are planted based on soil and water report, the quantity of water discharged by a bore well, the quality of water during summer also matters because simply mulching does't helps in solving the shortage of water problem becuase grape requires 10,000 to 15000 litres of water per day per acre. While filling the trenches the top soil should be filled at bottom upto a height of 2' depth, FYM 20 kg/ plant, 500 gm super phosphate, 100 gm Urea , SOP 100 gm, 200 g magnesium sulphate, 10 mg micronutrient per running foot, the remain trench is filled with down surface soil and levelled, some time neem leaf, or castor cake Glycerdia leaves are also applied.

Pour the water after filling the soil in the trench, this helps in easy permeable of water, soil becomes loose, good aeration the root stock penetrate better in soil because they produce good mass of roots, further they can apply with humic acid for root growth. The direction of the trench are not important if viens are proposed to train on pendal system (Bower system). But if the vines are proposed to train on GDC (Y) (Geneva double curtain) then North-South directiosn are important, this can also minimise the sun burn of the bunches under sub-tropical regions. E-W planting should be avoided. JCB are utilized to open the trench in rocky soil with 2½ bucket.

The best season of planting is February to March, when the temperature starts rising. The pits of 15x15x15 cm are opened in the trench at a spacing of 5' (10 x 5'), 4' (8' x 4'), 6' (12' x 6') 4' (6' x 4') etc. After planting the root stocks, press the soil and watered immediatly. If the polybags raised plants are there then the packets with sharp blades without damaging the ball of earth and put in the pit and press the soil and apply chloropyriphos to control the termites.

After planting light frequent irrigation rather than heavy application since the feeder roots are at the top only, then apply water based on evapotranspiration loss with 4 litre/hour discharge if Electricity availability is better if not, then it is given only for 4-6 hours then 8 litre discharge/Hour may be utilized or diffuser may also be utilized, and the drippers are placed at 2' distance.

After 15 days (16-30 days) of planting give urea 1kg/AC/ once in two days for 15 days 19:19:19 from 30-45 days 2 kg/ AC/ once in two days, urea 1kg/Ac/once in two days (46-60 days), 19:19:19 2 kg /AC/day once in two days (61-75 days) Urea 2 kg /Ac/once in two days (76-90 days), 19:19:19 2 kg/ AC/once in two days (91-105 days) Urea 2 kg/AC/once, 13:0:46 or 1:47:35, 2 kg/AC/Once in two days (121-150 days), 0:0:50, 2kg/AC/once in two days (151-180 days) other wise after 30 days of planting apply 25 kg urea, 15 kg DAP per acre and after 60 days of planting apply 25 kg urea per acre, after 90 days of planting apply 20 kg urea + 25 kg of SOP/AC and after 120 days of planting apply 25 kg of SOP/AC.

The roots stocks not susceptible to diseases like anthracnose, powdery mildew, down mildew however, root are not resistant to rust and alternaria disease, therefore, to control rust spray Kavach (Chlorothalonil 2gm/lit., Macozeb 2gm/lit, Tridemefone 1gm/lit, Alternaria can be controlled by spraying copper oxy chloride (Blitox) copper hydroxide (Kocide) 2 gm/lit. The chaffer beetles are serious in attacking the root stock which can by controlled by spraying Lanate (Methomyl) 1gm/lit. or Carbaryl 2gm/lit of water.

The root stocks are allowed to grow for 2 months which help in conserving the food, after 2 month weak thin shoots are removed, by maintaining 2-3 good shoots, generally two shoots are maintained for grafting Bamboo sticks are erected in each basin & they should be applied with tar (Dambar) to avoid attack of termites, in due course of time the leaves are removed at 15 days interval. The graftable diameter of the shoot should be 6-8 mm by September October and by October sap flow will be good for formation of dead parenchyma cells (Callus) and success of the graft. A temperature of 35°C and relative humidity of 75% has been found the best for good grafting for successful grafting trained malis (gardners) should be engaged for grafting α usually they charge one rupee each for grafting. By virtue of some problem if grafting fails immature green shoots are utilized for grafting during next June month, sometime if two-tier system (4-arm Kniffin system) is to be followed, then at bottom layer wine varieties can be utilized (viz. shiraz, pinot Noir, Zinfendal, Cabernet savignon, merlot etc.) & on top any table variety viz Thompson seedless, Flame seedless, Sharad seedless sonaka, Manik chaman, Tas-A-Ganesh Red globe, Crimson red are used.

The scion of any commercial table variety Thompson seedless, Manik Chaman, Tas-A-Ganesh, Sonaka, Sharad seedless, Red globe may be selected which is free from any disease, the scion stick should have short internodes with 9-12 months of age and 3-4 nodes and drenched in 0.1% carbendazim for 2-3 hours to avoid Botrydiplodia disease which subsequently kills the plants after grafting.

In insitu grafting wedge shape scion inserted into the slit open vertically on root stock and tie with polythene film, at a height of 1½' above the ground level, the grafting should not be done close to the ground level otherwise because of contact with irrigation water rotting of grafting union takes place and some time laboures while weeding also damage the grafted plant. The scion and root stock selected may be same thickness for good union. Some time it is difficult to get both mature scion and root stock. It is always better to select both mature scion and root stock.

There is lot of demand for grafted plants in grape which are available in polybags, by which the time required to raise the root stock and in situ grafting maybe reduced. The lacuna in grafting in polybag are the root stock thickness may not attain 8 mm and it will not be possible to graft at 1½' above the ground level, and there is a possibility that roots may get damaged after transplanting it is costly. So farmers prefers to go for in situ grafting which is cheap & best some time in grape because of in compatability between scion and root stock inverted bottle neck are formed this is due to uneven growth in both scion and root stock. This condition results in low yield after 4-5 years of grafting.

At certain occassion October grafting fails under such situation green wood grafting is done in May-June but the scion should have good food reserve. The other method of grafting is by chip budding, this is more easier in summer because of better sap flow and slippery bark and easy bud availability.

Better management and care is required to irrigate at proper time to see that the buds should not dry, equally better care is required to avoid damage near the joint or graft union. The grafting taken at a time but formation of union may take different time, so after Feberuary bottom cut is taken above the graft union, this helps in uniform growth. Based on the training system selected say Bower system. Telephone system, 4-arm Kniffin system, Single stake system, Y-Trelliss, Geneva double curtain system, develop the permanent frame work. Selection of training system is very very important because in Thompson seedless there is apical dominance problem exists which is more predominant in bower system, the cane develops horizontally and due to over lappig & shade, sprouting of buds is very difficult, such situations are easily over come by California System (Y-Trellis) which is a split canopy and low head system, where as Bower system or pendal system is high head and close centre.

Harvesting of sunlight from Eastern and Western side is very easy in Y Trellis system of training.

After grafting proper irrigation, pest & disease control is very important and loosening of polythene strips tied around the graft region to avoid girding of the stem. As soon as the plant reaches a height of 120-140 cm head back the plant &allow apical shoots to grow in the E-W directions. These will form primaries & allow to grow to a length of 30-45 cm and nip the apical portion allow two apical buds to grow from each primary area in N-S direction, this will form 4 cordons, when they attain 90 cm length again nip or pinch off, develop canes on cordon & develop 5-6 canes / 9 feet^2 this take 12 months to develop the frame work of the plant. Afterwards allow one cane/ft^2 after back pruning and restrict the shoot length to 4 feet after July till october pruning or fore pruning, during July-August take up cycocel spray at 250-500 ppm conc.to reduce the vigour of shoots to increase maturity otherwise spray KH_2PO_4 10gm/litre of water if April pruning delayed.

After October pruning keep two shoots/cane and arrange the shoots at 40-50 angle to the ground for better harvesting and keep only healthy canes, because the thin canes grow vertically and have more apical dominance. Maintain single stem rather than double stem, because single stem helps in reducing the diseases it also advisable initially to show cordon or primary arms, double cordons immediately in first year is not advisable because it reduces food reserve resulting in poor growth also it reduces the thickness of main stem. So by 2nd year of foundation pruning, the shoot at the basel node of the first year cordon may be turned into other side as another cordon thus this way we can develop double cordon and increase yield can be obtained. The length of cordon should be 2.5 to 3 feet, if the length increase apical dominance increases resulting in poor growth.

It is also advisable to maintain 2' in less vigrous varities and 2½' in vigrous varities between the codon, during summer burning of primary is observed if spacing is more than 2½' between two cordons & build micro climate and aeration will be affected.

In Tropical and sub-tropical region bud break is not a major problem during back pruning but it as a major problem in fore pruning the reasons are lack of chilling buds, poor cane maturity, low temperature after pruning and higher rate of apical dominance. Early cane bending, twisting used to follow which is cumbersom but now a days application of Hydrogen Cynide 1.5%, Thio urea 4.5% potassium Nitrate 4.5%, pactobutrazol 1000 to 1500 ppm by swabing to increase the fruit fullness of basal buds or lateral buds and to increase cluster cane ratio one has to go for sub-cane. After April pruning the buds starts sprouting and shoots develops into cane and there will be differnt growth rate some time vigrous, moderately vigrous. At 5th leaf stage spray cycocel 1 ml/lit. to 2 ml/lit of water to check the growth. When the vigrous shoots attains 10-11 leaves pinch at 9th leaf stage with 7-8 mm thickness. The moderatly vigrous shoots. When attain 8-9 leaf stage pinch 7th leaf, when less vigrous shoots of 4-5 mm thickness attain 6-7 leaf stage pinch at 5th leaf stage. Later new shoots appears from the apical buds which are designated as sub-canes. After maturity the sub-canes and apical canes are pruned at 3rd - 2nd, 1st leaf stage on vigrous, moderatly vigrous, less vigrous canes. This kind of sub-cane development helps in overcoming the bud-break after October pruning.

Application of nutrient helps in increased yield and quality, the requirement of nutrient also vary according to growth stage based on the growth select the fertilizer. Root stock plays an important role in uptake of nutrient as compared to on their own root.

Before the production starts apply more of nitrogen and low quantity of phosphorus and potash which also vary depending on soil type. So apply ½ kg super phosphate 100 g urea, 100 g SOP, once in 3 moths with ½ kg Neem cake and 10-15 kg FYM.

After attaining the fruit bearing stage apply the NPK in following manner. As Grape requires 660:880:660 kg /year and apply the fertilizer in three split doses both at April α October pruning. At April pruning apply 20% N, 60% P_2O after 30 days 20% N, 40% P_2O_5, 20% K_2O at 75 days after october pruning for Thompson seedless variety and its mutants viz. Tas-A-Ganesh Sonaka, Manikchaman, Clone -III.

Application of fertilizer viz urea, phosphoric acid, sulphate of potash can also be applied through drip. After April pruning NPK/kg/Ac/day is as follows. For one month 1.50 kg N, 1.4 kg P_2O_5 2nd month, 0.50 kg N, 2.0 kg P_2O_5, 0.45 kg K_2O/AC/Day, 3rd month 1.40 kg N, 1.40 kg K_2O/Ac/ day and at 4th month apply 0.40 kg K_2O/Day/AC.

The recommended dose of 275, 368, 275 kg of NPK/AC/ year, 30-40% can be saved by Fertigation. The dose to be given through Fertigation is 180:250:200 kg/AC/Year.

Based on petiole analysis exact nutrient recommendation on grape is possible Research done at various research stations recommends critical limits of the various nutrients elements for grape cultivation. If petiole analysis reveals more concentration of the nutrients than the critical level then fertilizer applied is more and if it is less then it is deficiently applied.

Root stocks shows deficiency symptoms of micronutrients like Mg, Mn & Zn because of more vigorus growth, so apply Zinc sulphate after 35 days of October pruning as foliar spray. Apply 50 gm MgSo4 per plant as soil application. At monthly inerval after blooming apply 0.15 to 0.25%.

Grape irrigation can be based on evapotranspiration of that area and farmers think that root stock do not require much irrigation, thinking that they have deep root system and absorb thin film of water also. Some time Tensiometer can be installed to see the requirement of water to see proper growth, fruit bud differentiation and yield. As in maize cultivation sunflower plants are used as indicator plants, in Grape also there is a need to develop indicator plants. It is better to irrigate before it show the stress symptoms like wilting of leaves in afternoon, proper irrigation after back pruning to get good growth is very important so better to apply light irrigations at frequent intervals than applying more water, some time mulching, spraying PMA, Kaoline, anti-stress also help to over come water demand.

Application of more water affect the soil health because it contain salts and in due course of time soil becomes saline which will leads to poor aertion less in filteration, water logging etc. Subsequently root rotting takes place. By drip irrigation 25% of irrigation water can be saved and yiled can be incresed by 30-45%. The wetting of soil depend on its texture, the sandy soil will have more infilteration rate & wetting area is deeper where as in case of clay/Black soil the rate of infilteration is lower and wetting area is shallower broader.

If the canopy area is 4m^2 the emitters should be 40 cm away from stem < the wetting area with the 50 cm and keep 2 emitters/vine. If the canopy area is 2m^2 than put emitters 30 cm away from the stem put 2 emiters/vines.

Depending on evaporanspiration rate in Norther Karanataka the water inputs by drip irrigation is as follows.

Complete harvest before 10 days of pruning and apply 18000 to 20,000 litre of water/AC/Day, 1-40 days after April pruning apply 20,000 to 24,000 lit./Day/AC, 40-70 days, 10,000 to 12,000 lit/Day/AC. From 71 day till October pruning 12,000 to 14,000 litrs/Day/AC. At October pruning from the day of October pruning to 40 days 16000 to 18000 litre/Day/AC at 41-75 days 10,000 to 12,000 litre/Day/AC, then 76 to 110 days of October pruning 18000 to 20,000 litres/Day/AC after 110 days till harvest 14000 to 16,000 litres/Day/AC.

In Grape major diseases are Anthracnose Downy mildew, powdery mildew. The root stocks viz. *Vitis champini, Vitis rupestris, vitis berlandieri, Vitis riparia* are resistant to diseases and these are used in breeding of root stocks like salt, Greek, St. George 1613, Dogridge etc. However necessary precaution are necessary when diseases are observed.

Rust is noticed in Bangalore blue variety where as root stocks are susceptible to rust.

To control Downy mildew spary Bordeux Mixture @ 0.5% copper oxy chloride 2.5 gm to 3 gm/lit. of water. Metalaxyl 2gm/lit. of water Ridomi MZ 2-2.5 gm/ lit.

To control powdery mildew, spray Bayletan 1gm/lit, Mancozeb 2.5 gm/lit, Karathane 0.25 ml/lit. of water, wettable sulphur 2gm/lit, miclobutanol 10WC, 0.5-1gm/lit or Hexaconozol + captafol 1.5 gm/lit.

To control Anthracnose spray Hexaconozol/1ml/lit, Thiophenate methyl 1 gm/lit of water, 1% Bordeux mixture, copper oxy chloride 2.5 to 3 gm/lit - copper Hydroxide 2gm/ lit.

Salt Creek root stock helps in improving sugar content in Thompson seedless. To maintain leaf and fruit ratio, one has to maintain a leaf area of 2500 cm^2 i.e. 12-15 leaves per bunch, other wise quality of the bunch will be deteriorates.

Girdling at 60 days after october pruning helps in fruit development by hendering the translocation of carbohydrate above the girdling zone. After October pruning following schedule helps in improving the bunch quality

(a) At April pruning at 5-7 leaf stage spray 250-500 ppm-CCC

(b) Spray GA - 15 ppm at pre-bloom

(c) Spray GA - 20 ppm at 25% cap fall

(d) Spray GA - 25 ppm at 25% cap fall

(e) Spray GA - 50 ppm at 100% cap fall

(f) Spray 6BA - 1--15 ppm at berry softening

(g) Spray NAA - 20 -25 ppm 25-20 days before harvesting to reduce berry shattering.

Chapter 6

April Pruning

April pruning: Why and how to do it:

The necessary information; Grape is cultivated in the Mediterranean region where the climate will be just like a coastal region. Under such a situation the grapevine grows continuously. Warm and dry weather is ideal for growth. It is successfully grown in southern parts of the country where the temperature ranges from 15° C to 40°C and annual rainfall amounts to over 50 cm. The amount of rainfall is not the criterion but the distribution is important for its successful growing. The rainfall should not coincide with the fresh growth after pruning or during fruit ripening, cloudy weather, high humidity, low temperature and precipitation. During flowering and berry development it is detrimental as they are highly infectious diseases.

After April pruning, to get 16-20 branches or canes, it requires 30-40 days and to establish the flower primordial it requires another 25-30 days. It means 50-60 days before the onset of monsoon, April pruning should be done; if the pruning gets delayed, the period available from April pruning to the onset of monsoon gets delayed which results in the immature cane growth and coincides with the rains and ultimately gets affected by anthracnose. The farmers are advised to take up KH_2 PO_4 10 g/litres of water to bring immediate maturity to the canes. In Karnataka the South West monsoon starts from 15th June and if the farmers take the pruning in the first week of April, the time available to develop a cane will be 10 weeks, by which time the canes get copper coloured and the wood gets matured and which results in minimizing the anthracnose problems. Further if pruning gets delayed by one week then the time available will be 9 weeks. Under water stress situation, they are advised to go in for anti-stress spray in the summer to overcome watershortage problem.

It has been experimentally proved that the most fruitful part of Thompson seedless variety is during the middle portion i.e., 6th to 9th node and accordingly the spur pruning or cane pruning is to be done.

Soil management:

To start with the soil, where vineyard have been established, it should be fertile and productive. Soil should be of good depth with good drainage having minimum lime content. The vineyard soil should be uniform. Any shortcoming should be avoided before planting, keeping the soil in good health. The fertility level should be checked every year. During the productive season the soil should have the following characters:

1) pH 6.7 to 7.7

2) Organic carbon– around one per cent

3) Electric conductivity – less than 20 mm hos/cm^2

4) Calcium carbonate – Less than 8 per cent.

5) Water-holding capacity – around 50 per cent.

Spacing, Primaries and Number of canes/vine

Spacing	Spacing in sq. foot	Number of primary	canes on each primary	Total cane
6' x 4'	24	2	8-10	16-20
8' x 6'	48	3	10-12	30-40
10' x 5'	50	3	10-15	40-50
10' x 6'	60	3	15-20	50-60
10' x 10'	100	4	20-25	80-100
12' x 8'	96	4	20-22	80-90
12' x 6'	72	4	15-20	60-70
12' x 4'	48	4	12-15	40-50
10' x 4'	40	4	8-10	35-40
8' x 8'	64	4	10-12	60-65

April Pruning:

While taking up the April pruning one should have full

knowledge about various year yield; based on that the future course of action depends upon the quality of the grape bunch existing in the previous years also reflected from the soil and water quality, the nutrition management and the pest and disease management, the proper and timely use of Hormones. On an average 10-12 tonnes per acre yield is expected if the yield is reduced by 10 per cent for various reasons as listed below:

1) After last April pruning new growth was not proper.
2) After October pruning flower production was not proper.
3) Proper attention was not given regarding flower formation and precautionary measures like spraying of 6BA - 10 ppm, 1AA - 10 ppm, NAA - 10 ppm was not taken.
4) Last October pruning canes had not matured.
5) There might have been disease and insect problem for which precautionary sprays were not taken up.
6) Natural calamities also caused loss of crop viz, hail storm, continuous rainfall and cyclone etc.,
7) The yield loss due to various reason needs to be examined for which precaution measures were taken.

Water and soil testing:

After the previous crop harvest by soil testing, one has to take two soil samples by digging one cubic feet pits and by scratching the soil from the inner surface of the pit it should be examined whether it is feasible for various nutrients and micronutrients. This is how the farmers will examine the crop yield to ascertain and implement the recommendation after analysis.

Watering:

After the harvesters of the previous crop give heavy watering or flooding. the previously fertilizer and excess sodium akalinity could have get accumulated in the plot, thereby leaching was made possible by flooding. After that soil testing should be taken up.

Inter-cultivation:

Once after heavy flooding, if the soil is ready for ploughing, take up deep ploughing, then collect the weeds especially hariyali and Jek *Cynodon dactylon, Cyprus rotundus.*

Application of Fertilizer:

Based on the soil report, application of fertilizer should be taken up usually by applying fertilizer as mentioned in the table for ready reference to the farmer.

Sl. No.	Name of the fertilizer	Fertilizer requirement per acre
1	Compost	12 tonnes
2	7:10:5	300 kg
3	DAP (18:46)	50 kg
4	Bio-fertilizer	15 kg
5	Micronutrient	15 kg
6	Bombaymeal	1 tonne
7	Magnesium sulphate	15 kg

Management of April Pruning:

By keeping the main stem and primaries-pest and disease -affected branches and weak branches from last season should be removed keeping them at a proper distance by keeping 1-2 buds and wherever the number of canes are more on the primaries then throw them out. If there are dried swollen/ barren region at the internodes region, then cut them from the bottom without leaving any stub. In 6' x 4', keep two primaries and 7-8 canes be maintained, with maximum of 12 canes on each primary.

Timely Pruning:

Before the rain starts and after completion of harvesting of the crop the April pruning is so adjusted that at the time of the beginning of the monsoon, the canes should have 14-15 leaves. If harvesting gets completed by the end of March then pruning is possible by mid-April. Then onwards 1½ to 2 months time is available for cane maturity. During April the temperature will be of 40°C and humidity would be very low. Hot wind will be blowing and the soil would also be having less nutrient after the crop harvest.

Therefore, based on soil analysis report apply only fertilizer to the soil to get proper growth otherwise the canes will be unproductive. One should not compromise with fertilizer application at the time of cane growth, as the loading of fertilizer gets accumulated in the stem before the new growth starts. If there is going to be any mistake, it will reflect on the yield. In case you want to go for sub-cane, allow the cane to grow up to the 6th bud and pinch the buds from the 6th bud and allow another 7 buds to grow. In another method allowing the cane to grow up to 8th bud, pinch the 8th bud and retain 7 buds. Then allow another 5 buds to grow and in both the cases the total number of leaves should be twelve.

So by June first fortnight complete the operation.

Management of Hormonal Practices to be adopted after April Pruning:

April Pruning	CCC	6 BA	Uracil
Pruning before 10th of April	500 ppm. at 5th leaf	-	-
April pruning between 10th-25th	1) 500 ppm at 5th leaf stage	20 ppm after 45 days of April pruning.	50 ppm. 45 days after April pruning.

April Pruning	CCC	6 BA	Uracil
	2) 750 ppm 7+5 leaf stage.		
April Pruning after 25th	1) 500 ppm at 5th leaf stage.	20 ppm,. after 5 days.	1) 50 ppm. after 45 days.
	2) 750 PPM 7+4 leaf stage		2) 50 ppm. after 55 days.
	3) 750 ppm at 7+4+4 leaf stage.		

Drenching of Bordeaux Mixture:

After hard pruning, drenching of Bordeaux mixture is necessary; one has to spray on the primaries and secondly one has to apply Bordeaux paste.

Important works to be taken up at April Pruning:

1) Take up April pruning in time
2) Before pruning take up inter-cultivation and apply fertilizer and water.
3) After April pruning, pasting of Bordeaux and application of lime to the main stem is necessary.
4) Disease affected, stem borer should be eradicated as its precautionary measures.
5) Testing of soil and adopting the recommendations.
6) After harvest vine should not be disturbed for 15 days. Undertake April pruning by 10th.
7) Apply 20 tonnes of farm yard manures, one tonne bone meal, 20 kg nitrogen and 60 kg phosphorus.
8) About 4-20 days after April pruning, flea beetle control is necessary by spraying Alphamethrin 1 ml/liter.

9) Keep one cane for every one square foot area at the 4-6 leaf stage and remove the thin canes.

10) At 5th leaf stage, spray 500 ppm Lihocin (1ml./litre)

11) 25 to 30 days after April pruning, apply 30 kg nitrogen and 40 kg phosphorus.

12) At 9th leaf stage, keep 7 leaves and pinch the small two leaves.

13) Spray 500 ppm, Lihocin (2nd spray) at 12 leaves (7+5 stage). Means when the cane is pinched at 7th leaf, it attains another 5 leaves.

14) After April pruning at 45 to 50th day, apply 50 kg potash.

15) About 40 -50 days after pruning, reduce irrigation.

16) Grow green manure crops viz., sunhemp in the month of July. If the soil is black then grow Dhaincha.

17) In September (1st week), cut the Sunhemp and apply to soil up to ½' depth and cover it.

Control of Pest and Disease:

After April pruning, due to hot climate, the occurrence of disease will be less. But to control mealy bug, flea beetle, leaf eating caterpillar, and mites one or two sprays are required.

1) Carbaryl (3g). or Malathion (2 ml); In the month of June when the monsoon starts, the leaves and canes get matured, that is, within 6-8 weeks diseases like Anthracnose, powdery mildew begins in the, first and third weeks. In that case Bordeaux mixture of one per cent foliar spray is necessary. Then in the months of July, August and September with 12-18 days gap, follow the following spraying schedule:

   First spray - Carbendizm of 1 g/lit quantity.

   Seconds spray - Captaf of 2 g/lit quantity.

   Third spray - Blitox of 2 g + streptocyclin ½g/litre quantity.

Fourth spray - Ziram 4ml /Liter

Use Apasa 80 0.25 ml/liter or any other sticker and if drizzling starts burn sulphur and apply its smoke.

Anti-Stress and its use in Grape Cultivation:

If there is a problem of irrigation due to water shortage then watering is important because at the flower primordial stage sufficient water quantity is a must. If there is a shortage of irrigation water, use of anti-stress is very important. When Anti-stress is mixed with water and sprayed, it will not be visible to the naked eye because it forms a very thin layer and from this layer water loss from the leaf will be minimized and the vine will not face water shortage.

The stomata on leaves stops loss of water to some extent, because of which CO_2 and oxygen exchangeability is not affected; the mites and jassides are controlled because of thin layer of anti-stress. Germination also gets minimized but new bunch and small berries are affected because anti-stress are not protected. The bunch, when gets soft, anti-stress should not be used, that is, when we use more water for irrigation the vine from roots absorb more water which gets filled in berries and because of less transpiration loss the berries get cracks and bunch starts rotting.

Schedule of Anti-Stress After April Pruning:

Sl. No.	Stage bunch	Anti-Stress/lit.
1	After April Pruning at 30th day.	2 m/lit.
2	After April Pruning at 55th day.	3 m/lit.
3	After April Pruning at 80th day	3 ml/lit.
4	After April Pruning at 105th day	4 ml/lit.
5	After October Pruning at 25th day	2 ml/lit.
6	After October Pruning at 55th day.	3 ml/lit.

Micro-nutrient Application After April Pruning

Time	Fertilizer Grade	Quantity
First spray June 15th	Micnelt - MS 32	500 gm in 100 lit (250 lit/AC)
Second spray July 15th	Fertilon combi - F	100 gm in 100 litre of water (250 litre/AC)
Third spray	Multiplex	250 ml in 100 lit of water (250 lit./AC)
Fourth spray	DAP + magnesium sulphate	(250 lit. per acre) 1.5 kg + 1/2 kg/500 liter

Water Management After April Pruning (Litre/AC/Day)

State	On own root	With Mulching	Mulching + anti-stress	Root-Stock	Anti-stress + rootstock
10-20 day before April pruning	0	0	0	0	0
Between 3-10 days of bud sprouting	19,200	17,600	17,600	13,000	12,000
Cane development stage of 11-35	24,000	22,000	14,400	16,000	12,000
Establishment of flower primordia 36-70 days	12,800	11,800	7,800	9,000	6,500
Bud development stage 71-100 days	15,000	14,000	10,500	10,000	8,000
Cane maturity stage 101-150 days	9600	9000	6800	8000	6,600

Water Management

There is a wrong assumption among the farmers that rootstock gardens do not require irrigation at normal and regular intervals. In fact rootstock can use the applied water more efficiently penetrating their roots into deeper layers, and they even absorb the film of water around the soil particle and save water to some extent.

Hence irrigation is most necessary for enhancing vine growth, fruit bud differentiation and production.

Points to be considered for efficient water management:

1) Irrigate the vines before they start showing symptoms of moisture stress like temporary wilting of leaves in the afternoon.

2) During summer irrigate the vines adequately to meet the evapo-transpiration requirement.

3) Plan the irrigation schedule meticulously to obtain rapid shoot growth in the initial stage; after April pruning it slows down its growth in the later stage to attain cane maturity and fruit bud differentiation.

4) Light and frequent irrigation are better than heavy and less frequent irrigation depending on soil type and availability of water.

5) Practice moisture conservation, like mulching anti-transpirant, spray and addition of sufficient organic matter into the soil to increase water use efficiency.

Excess Irrigation and Effects:

Excess irrigation than the required amount has adverse effect on soil characteristics which in turn affects plant growth and productivity. Since water contains one or other dissolved salts, excess irrigation leads to build-up of salts which in later years converts normal soil into saline soil. Also excess irrigation leads to poor infiltration resulting in water logging which affects soil aeration and roots start rotting leading to ultimately death of vines.

Drip Irrigation:

This is the most effective way of irrigating vine yards where the vines are irrigated frequently and slowly through emitters or various discharges. It also saves about 25% irrigation water and increases yield by 35-40 per cent than in basin irrigation.

Placement of Emitters:

The number of emitters to be fixed around each vine depends on the distance at which the emitters are fixed and the diameter of wetted area around each emitter (20-30 cm deep layer) in the soil. The weting of soil depends on its texture and water holding capacity. Rate of infiltration is faster in sand soils and in wetted area it is deeper. Whereas in clay soil rate of infiltration is slower and wetting area is shallower and broader. The number of emitters and its placement for seedless cultivars of grape is shown below:

Canopy area (m2)	Location of emitters from stem (cm)	Diameters of Wetted area (cm)	No. and location of emitters/vine
4-5	45	60	2 on line
2-3	30	60	2 on line

Irrigation Schedule:

Grapevine need water in different quantities during different growth stages Accordingly one should irrigate the vineyards. The quantity of water to be irrigated depends on the evaporation and transpiration rate. Based on the replenishment of evo-transpiration rate, water input by drip irrigation is as follows:		Water kilo liter/AC/Day	
Sl. No.	Stage	South Interior Karnataka	North Karnataka
1	From harvest to 10 days before April pruning	16-18	18-20
2	10 days before pruning to pruning	0	0
3	1-35 days after April pruning	18-20	20-24
4	36-70 days after April pruning	10-12	10-12
5	71 day after April pruning till October pruning	12-14	12-14
6	0-45 days after October pruning	14-16	16-18
7	46-75 days after October pruning	10-12	10-12
8	76-110 days after October pruning	16-18	18-20
9	After 111 days till harvest.	12-14	14-16

Chapter 7

October Pruning Management

Importance of October Pruning

1) October pruning with prior planning
2) The plot where October pruning is going to take place should be divided into different blocks.
3) Note down the work to be attended before October pruning
4) Note down the work to be attended after October pruning
5) Keep developed canes and buds before going in for October pruning
6) Go for bud testing in the laboratory.
7) Pasting of buds should be done.

Note:

1) How to prepare black Bordeaux paste: Take half kilogram of copper sulphate plus lime 250 gm + 125 gm of Thiourea in 5 litres of water and smear the front 3 buds.
2) Take Dormax/Romax of upto 30 ml/liter of water and swab it on the canes leaving the backside 3 buds for uniform bud sprouting.
3) By application of black Bordeaux or Dormex the apical dominance is controlled.

Importance of October Pruning when and how to do it:

Before and after October pruning the details of work to

be done should be understood thoroughly.

In Karnataka, the October pruning is done by the middle of October and under changing climatic condition, sometime early sometimes late pruning, is advocated. By doing early or late pruning what effect it is going to have on the crop is also important and should be kept under check.

October pruning is very important in grape cultivation. In Karnataka grape harvest starts as early as January and completes by the first week of April. The grape harvested in January month is not sweet and for export the sugar-acid ratio should be between 35:1 to 40:1 which is a must and that is possible in the month of February and March and for this purpose October pruning has to be done in the first fortnight of October.

At present before undertaking October pruning two points are very important which one has to take into consideration. First is to get the highest yield possible and second is to get good market response in different parts of the country. To realize these things this pruning is advised between 15th September to 15th November. Sometimes if one gets higher yield the prices will be less. So, we can conclude that it doesn't make much sense but it makes difference in the total expenses and returns. Therefore to tap the moderate price in this market, early or late pruning in October doesn't make much of a difference.

In our places, from 15th November to the last week of December, cold winter temperature prevails. In severe cold temperature conditions, the bud sprouting is difficult, therefore, by 15th of October pruning should be initiated.

Following Points to be Considered:

1) Too early Pruning:

For European markets, export of grape has a good scope, when Christmas and New Year are the two occasions when demand is more and one may get good returns. For this purpose if grapes are to be made available then in the 3rd week of December and in order to make harvest possible, October pruning has to be done by the 15th of August. There are heavy rains in August, causes more pest and diseases affictions.

Early pruned grape coincides with low temperature and with shortened day it results in less sugar development and a greenish colour means good harvest.

2) Early Pruning for Suitable Varieties:

In our country the old varieties are grown at the same time viz., Kishmish Charani, Sonak, Manik Chaman are harvested 1-2 weeks earlier under this condition. TSS will be around 22 to 24% but for export TSS of 18% is required which is possible in these varieties.

3) Necessity of Hormones before October pruning :

When you decide to go for early pruning watering in time is necessary. If the leaves stalk/pedicel are good, then defoliation becomes difficult since the sap flow is continuous and good towards fruiting buds, which will have an adverse effect on new sprouting. Therefore before pruning when you are not removing leaves at that time hormonal spray use is advisable. Later on the sap flow gets slower and because of formation of abscission layer leaf fall takes place. For early pruning such sprays are advantageous, with manual defoliation getting reduced. Among the chemicals Thiourea, Potassium Nitrate upto 3 to 5% and hormones like Ethrel upto 39% Sl 1000 ppm. to 2500 ppm. Ie., 2.5 ml/litres to 6 ml/litres and foliar spray are required. For coloured varieties Ethrel and others like Thiourea and Potassium Nitrate is necessary with use of Ethrel in white varieties which increases pink berry problem–so avoid using Ethrel in Thompson varieties etc. Before you take up spraying of chemicals for defoliation if there is a problem of diseases, then take up fungicide spray and defoliate. Before pruning affected branches affected by insects shortage of water and alkalinity may shoot up defoliation; that means the defoliation is not natural; one should know the function of leaves, necessity of removing the leaves; the purpose of October pruning etc.,

Water management and October pruning:

Early Pruning brings early fruits on the vine usually in the month of February when water requirement is more. If there is less availability of water then less watering is given to the vines. For the production of grape, watering should not be reduced but if reduced then the weight of the bunches get reduced. Under such situations by doing early pruning early harvesting is possible but when water filling starts in the berries, and comes across with water stress, the quality of the berries gets impaired. In the month of April and May the demand for grape will increase in North India, and to take advantage of this, pruning has to be done early to bring grape early in the market with good weight and quality. During April-May the temperature will be high and hence water loss from leaves also will be more, hence it is suggested to use anti-stress (5 ml/litres) or anti-transparent Kaolin (4 g/litres of water) and as the availability of water comes down naturally the rise in the context of pH intrudes to tackle this problem.

If late pruning is done in November, due to of cold the sprouting also comes late in November and the required berry swells and gets reduced and to overcome this problem use of hormones and nutrients is advised.

If pruning is done in the beginning of October then the sprouting will come into force, therefore keep the canes with good bunch and remove the others.

Early marketing area:

For export of grape how much quantity you can produce that you have to decide for yourself, thereafter the area should be earmarked. At present 25-30 tonnes per hectare yields is expected. Therefore, one area you can earmark, and the corner area of thorny bushes should be separated; then make two divisions of the area with ½ an acre of blocks and while taking up October pruning proper planning is important.

Planning of October Pruning:

Keeping the future line of work, pruning is planned as follows:

1) Pre-pruning preparation
2) October pruning
3) Post-pruning preparation

12-Point Programme:

1) Applications of bio-gas starter solution
2) Inter-cultivation
3) Light irrigation
4) Application of compost
5) Removal of leaves
6) Application of fungicide/insecticides to control pest and diseases.
7) The farmers are advised to follow phytosantitation.
8) Taking up pruning work
9) Application of chemicals for uniform bud burst
10) Application of fungicides.
11) Light inter-cultivation.
12) Light irrigation.

About 1-7 pre-pruning work, 8-Actual October pruning, and 9-12 Post-pruning work, leading to a total of 12 points programme.

A Pre-October Pruning Programme:

Before you take up actual October pruning, the points mentioned above (1-7) should be taken into account. After deciding the dates of October pruning 22 to 25 days works should start before. If October pruning is to be taken in the first fortnight of October then 1 or 2 dates you have to fix up and if rains have occurred approximately 25 days early and are continuous, it will be congenial. If the garden soil is not good or the soil contains 8% lime nodules, then give heavy flooding to wash out the salts that are accumulated near the root zone, which is the main purpose of this programme of pre-October pruning.

Fertilizer Application:

Based on soil test the fertilizer should be applied as follows:

Sl. No.	Name of the fertilizer	Quantity/AC.
1	Compost	10 tonnes
2	Diammoniaum phosphate (DAP)	75 kg
3	Micronutrient mixture	20 kg
4	Magnesium sulphate	15 kg
5	Borocal	10-15 kg
6	Bio-inoculants	15 kg

Give irrigation, when the date of actual October pruning is over 4-6 days before and remove leaves from vine, as also weak canes, insect, disease-affected and thick canes. If the spacing of the garden is 8' x 6' then keep 40 canes i.e., 75% of the total canes.

Cleanliness: Collect all the fallen leaves and canes from the garden and burn them.

Foliar Spray: Disease and insect-affected branches should be given a spray of insecticide and fungicide. viz., sulphur dusting on plants and ground should be done.

B) Actual October Pruning

Keep the required buds on every cane and go for October

pruning. Try to understand the sub-cane metholdology which means if 5+7 buds system is allowed in April, during October pruning it should be pruned leaving about 7 buds. Whereas in case of 7+5, the pruning is done leaving 7 buds, which is referred to as zero pruning. In long canes we find 10 to 11 buds that are close to each other, which is a genetic make-up in Thompson seedless under this condition, the October pruning is done at the 11th bud. In general the 6th bud is most potential in Thompson seedless.

In case of 8' x 6' spacing, every grapevine should have 40 canes and on every cane 5th, 6th and 7th buds are most productive, then you will get 120 productive buds per vine. Out of which 50% buds sprout then you will get 60 bunches per vine. Usually you get 40% flowering then 45 bunches you are sure to get.

Spacing and number of buds/vine.

Spacing	No. of Canes/vine	Pruning at buds	Total No. of buds/vine	Good buds/vine
6' x 4'	20	6th bud	120	20
	18	7th bud	116	30
8' x 6'	40	6th bud	240	40
	36	7th bud	245	54
8' x 4'	30	6th bud	180	30
	24	7th bud	175	36
10' x 5'	40	6th bud	240	40
	36	7th bud	245	54
10' x 10'	80	6th bud	480	80
	60	7th bud	420	90

As per the schedule given above, approximately 12 tonnes per acre of yield are expected. If the number of buds are more, then upto15 tonnes/AC yield also can be expected.

C Post October Pruning:

For getting bunches in the same shoot the pasting of black Bordeaux is required. This paste is applied leaving the last 3 buds on the canes. Take half kg copper sulphate, 250 gm lime and 125 gm Thiourea in 5 litres of water and paste it on the canes. Secondly, Dormex (Hydrogen Cyanide) 30 ml/lit also can be swabbed by lint with handgloves.

After application of paste take up insecticide dusting on soil. Pruning work, pasting, and insecticide dusting should be done on the same day and after completion of all this on 2nd and 3rd day, light soil stirring is required and then irrigate.

After October pruning, or when the pruning work starts take to irrigation and after completion or pruning once again watering is given, so that this you can say October pruning work is over.

Usually from the 15th of September, first work should start and complete by 15th October this way in one month all operations will be competed of pre-pruning operation and other related works cannot be carried out simultaneously. But if the October pruning is done properly, it will have an impact on the percentage of flowering. If pruning is done, don't think work is over. Then good grape production is not possible. One acre pruning is done in one day, but later on we will come to know that out of one acre only ½ acre flowering is good which means the sprouting is uniform and flowering percentage is also good but in the remaining ½ acre area, sprouting was less hence flowerings are also less. Under such a situation why such a problem has arisen one has to think it over. Everytime one will think why it is so, inspite of October pruning done in time taken all precautions.

This point, if you take it to your mind in a proper way,

you will understand pre-pruning operation were not carried out properly hence good post–pruning results were not got. Only pre-pruning operation are not the reasons, the work carried out after April pruning one may have missed out something.

Development of cane, nipping of canes, application of fertilizers and watering work, all this work you divide into different sections from April pruning to October pruning and you keep in mind that every bunch should weigh around 500 gm and each berry should weigh around 4 gm. In case of 8' x 6' spacing, every vine should give 5 kg boxfull of production and the capability of each vine that you can see after October pruning, force it to flower and for that purpose October pruning management is very important.

Testing of buds before October Pruning:

Testing is it Necessary? Yes

Just to see how many flower primordias have got established and got confirmed.

When to test it?–10-15 days before October pruning.

Which buds to be tested?– Usually 6-7 buds.

Method of bud Testing?–Through microscope.

Without cane Pruning bud Testing: Remove all the leaves from the vine by doing pruning on matured canes and apply thiourea/Dormex after which 4 buds testing of cane is possible.

After October Pruning Pasting is necessary?

Yes it is necessary to raise such question at the time of pruning.

1) **Apical dominance:** At apical region the dominance is more to overcome that, application of Thiourea or Dormex is necessary.

2) During October pruning, reduction in temperature during

winters may cause slow sprouting of buds and uniform growth is not possible, by 15th October if there is heavy rainfall coinciding with pruning, delay in sprouting is caused and with soil affected by lime nodules the moisture holding capacity may increase. Late pruning means last week of October or early November, that is, Ist week of November. Where there is reduction in temperature and less sunshine, delay in sprouting of buds may be caused.

3) If number of canes on the number of bud-load are more than expected then also the sprouting after October pruning gets delayed and it will not be uniform too.

4) The bud burst may vary from variety to variety. The variety Tas-e-Ganesh as compared to Thompson seedless, Sonaka and manik Chaman is more vigorous. In Kishmish Charani variety there is no apical dominance.

5) On canes, the lower 3-4 buds have lower establishment of flower primordia, which results in less flowering. It may be of any variety and in order to have sure shot sprouting it is compulsory that one has to go for pasting.

Which paste one has to select?

Application of Thiourea or black Brodeaux paste. And Dormex has shown not much difference in overcoming the apical dominance. But Thiourea percentage is controversial and before use of Dormex testing is also necessary. In some places, after the preparation of paste, they have to be applied immediately, sometime the application at the earliest possible may give good result. It is necessary that applied paste should be there for at least 5-6 hours on buds. After the application of paste, increase in temperature and the day length duration have a deciding effect on bud sprouting.

Post-paste Application and Other Points to Remember:

1) As per the programme to have uniform bud sprouting,

application of paste is necessary.

2) In Black Bordeaux mixture urea percentage should not be more than 3 per cent, and the Dormex percentage should not exceed 3%.

3) Once the paste is prepared, immediately it should be used.

4) Application of paste should start from afternoon 3 pm to 5 pm.

5) The paste should be applied on apical 2-3 buds only.

6) Use gloves while applying paste and use cloth brush.

(Courtesy Dr. B.G. Bhujabal, Drakshi Virut, Pune)

Chapter 8

Nutrition Management

Grape yield and nutrition management have close relationship and is very important; also it is the quantity which will have effect on quality and optimum fruit load which brings uniform sugar, acid ratio that ultimately decides the quality. In our place grape is cultivated but with two distinct pruning practices, i.e., April, to promote growth amd october purning for proudction of bunches to take every year high and quality production of grapes and nutrition management is very important.

Climatic Relationships/ Nutrition Management:

1) To get a good grape bunch, pruning is done between rainy season and winter. But in Karnataka we find three distinct phase of climate i.e.., summer, rainy and winter seasons. The establishment of flower primordia in grape takes place before winter but the development of bunch starts in winter; its ripening starts from the end of winter season. So it requires two different pruning methods to get the crop. If you think grape bunch development takes place in winter and its nutrition management, your work should be done in that period. In winter the development is slow compared to other seasons; during winters relative humidity and temperature are less but the light is medium. For the development of bunch three stages are required:

2) After pruning, sprouting, flowering, and bunch development for the establishment of flower; it requires 6 weeks.

3) After flower establishment, the berries and bunch development starts; it requires 6 weeks time.

4) Third stage of the development stops and the ripening period starts and to complete this stage it requires 6 weeks. It means from October pruning onwards from flowering to harvesting 4½ months time is required. For a good grape production as mentioned above in three or four stages the nutrition management in a very good manner is very important.

   1) First stage – sprouting, sprout development, flower production. It takes 4 weeks.

   2) Second stage – flowers bunch emergence, flowering, fruit set. It takes 4 weeks.

   3) Third stage – berry development, bunch development. It takes 4weeks.

   4) Fourth stage – Fruit ripening. It takes 4 weeks.

Overall it requires 4 months. For every stage of development that takes place right from leaf, flower and bunch onwards and other parts, one has to understand about nutrition activities.

Post-October Pruning First Stage:

Before October pruning remove all the leaves and prior to that the establishment of flower primordia, nutrients applied for the development of framework of the canes etc., is important. After October pruning emergence of new sprouts, new leaves, nutrient requirement, management of deficiency symptoms, depends on the availability of nutrients in the soil. The climate, NPK and trace element availability of water-all these factors are congenial, then sap flow starts. After vine canes are pruned, at cut portion the water starts coming out. If this situation is not observed then availability of water in root zone is less and air is more. One should understand that properly. That kind of situation i.e. increase in water and decrease in air at root zone does exist.

Third part is use of fertilizer and hormones. New growth that we call as white root hair growth are necessary, for that purpose phosphoric acid and uric acid and hormone -like indole acetic acid are required and in due course of time we see amino acid is produced in the soil. Very often farmyard manure and compost is required and use of green manure is equally important. The living organism plays an important role to work on green manure, so it should get well-mixed in the soil. Vermiculture and vermicompost difference one should keep in mind. Azotobacter, rhizobium, PSB, bio-fertilizer are available in the market. The availability of C:N ratio in soil is important. Therefore, before pruning and production of white root hairs, application of fertilizer and compost is equally important. After pruning early application of fertilizer will help in the improvement of soil nutrient.

After October Pruning 2nd Step:

At this stage new growth development and production of full leaves are observed and the leaves are green in colour with good leaf area and age of the leaves will be around 30 days; that means they are mature enough to do the job of photosynthesis; at the same time the sunshine hour helps the dormant bunch to develop, and in soil you may find depletion of nutrients. Suddenly the vines may show hungry symptoms as more nitrogen is required.

This situation is observed at the beginning of the 2nd step of October pruning i.e., 25-30 days of pruning; nitrogen requirement one has to fullfill completely, if nitrogen nutrient is applied early it will help the vine. Sometimes if nitrogen is applied in the beginning more nitrogen is available then it will have bad effect. How much nitrogen, in which form and in how many split doses through soil and foliar, one has to decide whether only nitrogen is to be applied or other fertilizer is to be applied.

Petiole analysis is a landmark in understanding the exact requirement when vigorous sprouting starts; 6th leaf or its petiole analysis is done for nitrogen, which maybe in the range of 1.5 to 2 per cent.

Based on Petiole Analysis Nitrogen Requirement:

Sl. No.	Petiole (N)	Per hectare N required	Per acre N required
1	2.5 and above	Nil	Nil
2	2.4 to 2.5	10 kg	4 kg
3	2.3 to 2.4	20 kg	8 kg
4	2.2 to 2.3	30 kg	12 kg
5	2.1 to 2.2	40 kg	16 kg
6	2.0 to 2.1	50 kg	20 kg
7	1.9 to 2.0	60 kg	24 kg
8	1.8 to 1.7	70 kg	28 kg
9	1.7 to 1.8	80 kg	32 kg
10	1.6 to 1.7	90 kg	36 kg
11	1.5 to 1.6	100 kg	40 kg
12	1.4 to 1.5	110 kg	44 kg
13	1.3 to 1.4	120 kg	48 kg
14	1.2 to 1.3	130 kg	52 kg
15	1.1 to 1.2	140 kg	60 kg
16	1.0 to 1.1	150 kg	60 kg
17	1.0 to 1.0	160 kg	64 kg

Means the nitrogen quantity you supposed to apply out of which 50% nitrogen at second stage you have to apply menas after 4 weeks 50%. Nitrogen you have to apply. This 50% quantity of N to be applied in two weeks for two times and every week 4 times if two times a week, 8 times . Alternate day 16 times or daily 28 to 32 times. If drip irrigation facilties available then apply through drip also.

Requirement of Magnesium alongwith Nitrogen:

For the production of Chlorophyll in leaves nitrogen is required but magnesium is equally important. Ammonium sulphate 100 kg + 15 kg magnesium sulphate together can be used or go for Petiole analysis to assess the magnesium sulphate requirement.

After October Pruning 3rd Step:

At this stage of fruit development the demand for nitrogen and phosphorus increases. At the beginning nitrogen and 0.4% phosphorus is required in the petiole. For that purpose the nitrogen quantity (remaining 50%) alongwith phosphorus should be applied. If the lime stone exceeds > 8-10% then apply 7:10:0 (500 kg) and if lime stone is medium in soil then apply 18:46 (DAP) fertilizer (100 kg) per hectare for 55 to 60 days; after October pruning this quantity you have to apply.

After October Pruning 4th Step:

At this stage the growth of leaves and fruits stops but ripening starts. The berry colour starts changing. To help this activity application of potash becomes necessary. About 75-90 days after October pruning, apply the required quantity of nitrogen, phosphorus, and potash or only potash.

Per hectare:

1 tonne compost (3-4 cart load)

+ 300 kg 19:19:19 and 125 kg sulphate of potash

Per Acre:

400 kg compost (1 cart load)

+ 300 kg 19:19:19 + 50 kg SOP

At this stage nitrogen should be applied in big doses. Application of nitrogen fertilizer should be stopped when the bunch starts ripening and the new growth starts. If you apply fertilizer early without potash (i.e., NP) it will have good effect on fruit development and early set bunch shows more water berry symptoms. So alongwith DAP or individual application of N & P add sulphate of potash. If you apply MOP it will affect the quality of bunch and if chloride is more in irrigation water, in such a situation apply sulphate of potash alongwith compost.

At every stage of application of fertilizer one has to keep in mind that at this stage which fertiliser is required, and how to fullfil the requirement.

Ist Stage – (one months) – nitrogen and magnesium

IInd Stage – (Two months) – nitrogen and phosphorus/ Urea Phosphate.

III rd Stage – (3 months) – nitrogen, phosphorus, potash/urea phosphate + potash – lastly potash.

Micro-nutrient Requirement

In grape nutrient management, NPK is very important but how to fulfil the requirement of NPK, in what form it should be applied are very important. Alongwith NPK, the secondary important nutrients viz., calcium, magnesium and sulphur are also equally important. In Karnataka the grape growers, among the secondary elements, use more of magnesium. If magnesium is applied in more quantity, more yield is expected; this has been impressed in the farmers mind and this is true also. It does't mean by reducing the required fertilizer or just skipping the application of fertilizer, one can expect higher yield. Most important is to understand the importance of secondary elements and how they help in increasing the yield. By micro-nutrient application (1) how to increase yield and (2) quality improvement; this understanding is important to farmers.

For grape development and yield all secondary elements are important. Every individual element effect is different viz zinc, iron manganese, copper, molybdenum and boron are also important. After October pruning, 4 steps are already discussed like the use of micronutrient are important during 2 and 3 steps, for leaves growth and fruit development etc., When leaves show symptoms of developing zinc and manganese deficiency these two are required in large quantity. At fruit stage ferrous and boron are required in large quantity. Copper is required at development stage and molybdenum is required at establishment of flower primordia.

Micronutrient Requirement:

Once ferrous and zinc deficiency are seen there is change in leaf colour. Boron and manganese deficiency have correlation with leaf shape and leaf colour to some extent. But, in flower/bunch, micro-nutrient deficiency is not visible. It may not affect the yield but hamper the quality. Therefore, it is a must to use micro-nutrient in grape cultivation.

After pruning the new growth when it emerges comes with force and sometimes slow growth is observed. Manganese and zinc deficiency results in slow growth. When the growth is not uniform there will not be uniform flower primordia establishment. The injury caused by pruning has to be healed. Otherwise some branches may die and the food has to be diverted to good and healthy canes which ultimately result in improper nutrition of bunch of berries. Boron deficiency causes improper fruit set. Fruit set will be early but slow and stops immediately, which affects the berries on vine, which set early, is slow growth. Early set berries becomes bigger and the late set berries becomes smaller in size and at the tip the shoot berries will be more. Leaf boron and molybdenum deficiency results in early filling of sugar which causes berry growth to stop and at ripening phase sink starts, and in some berries totally sugar filling wont takes place, which results in water berries and further reflect in mummification.

Lime Nodules Affects Soil and Micro-nutrients:

In Karnataka lime nodules are more in the soil and with soils having 8-10 % lime content, quality grape production becomes very difficult. Ferrous content of lime nodules will not be available to leaves and leaves show deficiency symptoms in younger leaves viz., the leaves will be whitish or yellowish in colour. This can't be helped, which further causes physiological disorders with the symptoms being observed on leaves only and on bunch or berries and later on, any precaution taken is not going to help.

Micro-nutrient Requirement:

If you get more yield then you won't get export quality. Per acre 10 tonnes or per hectare 25 tonnes yield is not important. If you get the produce of 25 tonnes what if it comprises 20-25% for export, the use of micro-nutrient becomes essential. For getting export quality, micro-nutrient, nitrogen, phosphate, potash, are used in a balanced manner. The requirement of micro-nutrient is felt at new growth whenever deficiency symptoms are exhibited; at the same time pinching is advocated; so one should not think that the problem is solved. At the time when major nutrient like nitrogen and potash for vigorous growth magnesium requirements becomes more under such situation micro-nutrients are also required in large quantity. If you apply then it will affect and reflect on quality.

Testing and Apply:

By petiole analysis the exact requirement of nutrients can be assessed and after diagnosis the period can be calculated. Simple soil analysis will not be helpful. If one has to go for leaf analysis which requires time and by which time when the critical vine requires nutrients it is late. Even then if we apply micro-nutrients and our orchard improves leaves may show improvement or they may resemble like improved ones but it will not reflect on bunch. If problem is noticed then micronutrients are required. Therefore advance application is always better.

Foliar application on leaves:

Alongwith soil bio-fertilizers, especially compost and green manures are applied and through that micro-nutrients requirement will be fulfilled to some extent but that will not be sufficient. One has to compensate through soil micro-nutrients. At both pruning stages application of micro-nutrients helps in improving the soil fertility reserve. Then application of micronutrient to leaves is not necessary. When the new sprouts come up, zinc. manganese, are required. At fruit development and ripening boron, molybdenum are required. Copper application is required as a catalyst but in lime-rich soils ferrous availability is improved by applying chelated form or manganese and zinc which are to be applied together. While doing foliar spray on leaves, first spray at sprouting, second spray when the bunch is in flowering stage, third spray at full fruit set and after spraying when the bunch is in flowering stage, spray at full fruit set and after girdling and if necessary, spray after third spray and the requirement of micro-nutrient is almost over. While you are going for spraying but by mistake if you apply, more there is possibility of chloride injury to leaves and when the bunch is in flowering stage micro-nutrient spray will be helpful in future.

Application of zinc, (30-40 ppm.) manganese (20-25 ppm.) ferrous (25-35 ppm,) is beneficial but excess boron is harmful; always apply in low concentration but you may not get the result and in early application of boron don't apply, it will not be beneficial.

1) Foliar application of different micro-nutrient by mixing

Schedule of Fertilizer After October Pruning for Higher Yield of Grape

Sl. No.	Time/Vine Care	By soil application/ hectare	By folir spray
1	3-4 Weeks after pruning/at new growth	Nitrogen 50 kg, Magnesium 5 kg,	Zinc, magnesium (50 to 100 ppm)
2	4-8 weeks after pruning, at bunch growth flowering, berry setting	Nitrogen 50 kg, phosphate 50 kg	Boron, zinc (75 to 150 ppm)
3	8-10 Weeks after pruning berry development	Nitrogen 50 kg, phosphate 50 kg, potash 50 kg	Ferrous copper (100 to 150 ppm)
4	10-12 weeks fruit ripening starts	potash 100 kg	Boron, molybdenum (150 to 220 ppm)

can be applied to leaves or ready-made mixture may be used.

2) Chelated micro-nutrient should be used with care.

3) Along with micro-nutrient hormones cannot be used.

4) While applying fertilizer through soil and foliar means, there should be some gap.

5) At flower primordia, by petiole analysis and as per diagnosis change the programme.

6) Once the bunch ripening starts stop using foliar sprays of micro-nutrient.

7) Every year this programme should not be changed on

large scale.

For every farmer to get a good quality grape, a proper beginning is necessary. Grape orchard should have drip irrigation facility and one should have detailed information about irrigation management.

Water Management by Drip:

Grape will be continuously growing throughout the year and that development has to take place in a proper manner and to get higher yield in grape two times pruning is done. First pruning in April and second pruning in October and later on the water requirement of vine from pruning is done to get full vegetative growth (canopy cover). Establishment of flower primordia to (60-120 days) harvest and again from October pruning till harvest are critical as different problems crop up. Therefore water management scheduling is very important.

Water Management Through Drip in Grape:

For grape cultivation one has to consider the following points while going in for drip irrigation:

1) Rate of Evaporation:

Daily how much evaporation loss has occurred is expressed as USWB class. A pan evaporimeter is used to measure it and it is expressed in mm/day and daily at 8:30 it is recorded. When drip is used for irrigation and by chance there is a rainfall and how much water is utilized for crop (effective rainfall) and its deduction is necessary. For example if rainfall is more than daily evaporation loss then irrigation is not necessary. If rainfall is less, then daily evaporation loss, from rainfall has to be deducted from daily evaporation loss and keeping in mind the balance in evaporation loss irrigation is taken up.

Requirement of Effective rainfall by drip irrigation

Day	Evaporation mm/day	Rainfall mm/day	Effective rainfall/(mm)	While irrigation consider evaporation loss (mm)
3.7.06	7.4	2.9	2.9	4.5
4.7.06	8.3	-	-	8.3
5.7.06	8.10	10.2	8.0	0.0

If the rainfall is more than expected, looking to soil condition, don't irrigate for 48 to 72 hours. Later on keeping in mind evapotranspiration loss and rainfall, go for irrigation.

2) Evaporation Factor:

There is little controversy about pan-evaporimeter because it is made up of iron sheet and it is influenced by the surrounding atmosphere/existing situation. If the level of water in pan-evoporimeter is less, it is considered that the loss of water will be more. In our situation the factor will be 0.7 to 0.8.

3) Yield Factor:

As the canopy spread advances, the requirement of water also advances. One square foot area should give 400g fruit from one bunch. One bunch growth requires 2600 to 2700 sq. cm of leaf area, means 6 x 4 foot distance in an acre have 1800 plants. And on every vine 25 bunches, with 400g weight, per acre 18 tonnes and per hectare 40-45 tonnes yield is expected. Hence the leaf area and water requirement have co-relation. As per FAO book on page number 24 to 33 detailed information is given for a new grape garden, the yield factor ranges between 0.25 to 0.95. But when the canopy is fully covered, on the pendals this factor from pruning to bunch emergency arises and for harvest 0.6 to 0.90 should be considered.

4) Wetting Area:

Through drip irrigation system, 30 per cent soil should be wet. On an average grape garden should have 60 cm. soil layer and it should hold 40% available soil moisture for getting good crop.

Water Requirement of a Grapevine:

Evaporation loss and role of evaporation factor will play an important factor in assessing the water requirement of a vineyard and how much water is required can be calculated by yield factor.

At micro-level/drip irrigation method how much water is required for a vine can be calculated by = A x B x C x D x E (litre/day)

A = Daily total evaporation loss (9 mm)

B = Evaporation factor 0.7

C = Grapevine growth factor

D = Grapevine yield /Sq. meter.

E = Soil wetting area (%)

(Note:) For Alternate day watering, two days evaporation loss has to be taken into account.

How Many Times Irrigation is Required:

Once you calculate the water requirement, later on for irrigation of grapevine, by drip irrigation how much we have to keep watering is very important.

$$\text{Drip irrigation time (Hour)} = \frac{\text{Vines total water requirement (liter)}}{\text{Discharge from one dripper (liter/Ha) per vine total}}$$

Meanwhile the field area measurement and how much drippers are required:

For Example:

A = Daily evaporation loss - 10 mm

B = Evaporation loss factor -0.70

C = Grapevine vine factor - 0.90

D = Vine spacing wetting are - 1.83 M x 1.22 M = 40 % = 0.40 one day

Water requirement/vine = One day evaporation loss x open pan evaporation. (mm) meter (litre/day)

Development stage x grape area (M^2) x wetting area.

Grape vine water requirement = 10 x 0.7 x 0.9 x 2.23 x 0.40 = 5.65 liter/day.

Different Buds of Evaporation, Grapevine Yield, Factors and water Requirement for Grapevine.

Evaporation Loss	Grape Vine Spacing (Square Foot)											
	6' x 4'				8' x 5'				10' x 5'			
	Yield Factor				Yield Factor				Yield Factor			
	0.6	0.7	0.8	0.9	0.6	0.7	0.8	0.9	0.6	0.7	0.8	0.9
3	1.2	1.4	1.5	1.7	1.9	2.2	2.5	2.9	2.4	2.8	3.2	3.5
4	1.5	1.8	2.0	2.3	2.5	3.0	3.4	3.8	3.2	3.7	4.2	4.7
5	1.9	2.2	2.5	2.9	3.2	3.7	4.2	4.7	3.9	4.6	5.2	5.9
6	2.3	2.7	3.0	3.4	3.8	4.4	5.0	5.6	6.6	5.5	6.3	7.0
7	2.7	3.1	3.5	4.0	4.5	5.0	5.6	6.6	5.5	6.4	7.3	8.2
8	3.0	3.5	4.0	4.5	5.0	5.9	6.7	7.5	6.3	7.3	8.4	9.4
9	3.4	4.0	4.5	5.6	5.7	6.6	7.5	8.5	7.1	8.2	9.4	10.6
10	3.8	4.4	5.0	5.7	6.3	7.3	8.4	9.4	7.9	10.5	11.7	-
11	4.2	4.8	5.5	6.2	6.9	8.1	9.2	10.3	8.6	10.0	11.5	12.9
12	4.5	5.3	6.0	6.8	7.5	8.8	10.0	11.3	9.4	11.0	12.5	14.9
13	4.9	5.7	6.5	7.4	8.2	9.5	10.9	12.2	10.2	11.9	13.6	15.2
14	5.3	6.2	7.0	7.9	8.8	10.2	11.7	13.9	11.0	12.8	14.6	16.4

Drip for how much time to keep?

One dripper/hour = 3.75 litre

Therefore, Drip running period hours = $\frac{5.65}{3.75}$ = 1.50 (One and half hour)

What Type of Dripper and How Many Drippers Required:

While fixing drippers the following points one has to take into consideration.

1) Dripper should be sturdy/durable
2) Dripper hole should be bigger because it won't get clogged.

How many dripper and which type is required depends on the type of soil, how much land to be wetted, light soil requires low out put dripper of 4 liter/hr. Two drippers on both the sides of vine and in a short time irrigation is made possible. But for medium and heavy soils, for one grapevine it requires one dripper of 4 liter/hour and it should be fixed at 20-30 cm apart. Between two vines one or two drippers at equal distance should be fixed. By dripper how much water is given the following table:

Relationship of Soil, Dripper and Wetting Area

Sl. No.	Type of soil	By dripper and horizontal area (cm)	Depth of Wet Soil (cm)
1.	Heavy	50-60	100-120
2.	Medium	40-50	80-90
3.	Light	20-30	40-50

The wetting area depends on the soil type, of dripper, method of quantity of irrigation of water applied, the distance between two dripper. The vertical 20-40 cm depth of wet soil is sufficient for grapevine. Excess watering helps in removing the salt from the soil, which moves the salt away from the soil. Overlap watering should be 20-30% as per the research findings.

For overlap watering **By dripper wetting area?**

(Distance between two dripper) = Meter x 0.7 to 0.80

Micro-irrigation by all methods can be given every alternate day and main reasons are if more than required time the vines are irrigated, the loose soil (water and air) is filled up which spoils the vines, water and air balance which results in non-availability of oxygen to vines. Therefore alternate day irrigation helps in reducing the disease also.

Pruning and Water management:

In grape, two time pruning is done, and at different stages of pruning, different water quantity is required and while giving irrigation by drip little changes are required.

April Pruning:

Once grape harvesting is complete grape garden should not be tampered for 8 days before April pruning and 10-15 days afterwards April pruning dripper should be stopped. The other work of the orchard can be attended to. Take up inter-cultivation, apply compost and bio-fertilizers. In the beginning, keep dripper for a longer time on soil to a saturation point and later drip irrigation x 0.6 is run on. After April pruning and after complete work is over, the grapevine requires less; water because number of leaves are less if watering is done more than the required amount then excess growth is observed. After pruning 30 to 60 days, the leaves growth hastens. During this period the flower primordia is established and at that time more watering is required and during this period more temperature, persists the evaporation loss through soil, the transpiration loss through leaves will be more, hence the quantity of water given should be increased. In afternoon, to suffice the water requirement, this period yields factor 0.75 that should be considered. Vine growth is very fast

Weeks after Pruning	Days after Pruning	Yield factor
1-2	0-15	0.60
3-4	16-30	0.75
5-6	31-45	0.90
7 and above	45 and above	0.90

and canopy is fully covered; in 60-80 days the flower primordia also gets developed. The following yield factor for irrigation should be followed:

October Pruning:

15th October is the best time for October pruning when the soil is too wet because then excess growth takes place. Therefore, for 8 days keep the drip closed after October pruning and later after 15 days the drip has to be kept open, 0.70 yield factor at 0.60 with light irrigation be given. Then after 20 days, 0.70 yield factor and then later for 25 days, by taking 0.80 yield factor, drip irrigation be given and when the water filling starts in berries from 75-80 days for that purpose by taking drip yield factor (0.9) the watering has to be continued. If watering is excess or less it leads to water berry and too much watering leads to bigger water berry and berries cracks, and rot. Once the harvesting is over stop drip irrigation. Follow the following drip irrigation chart as mentioned below:

Sl. No.	Weeks after October pruning	Day after October pruning	Yield factor
1	1	0-8	No watering
2	2 to 3	9-13	0.70
3	4 to 6	24-42	0.80
4	7 to 9	43-68	0.80
5	10 and above	61 and above	0.90

It looks that water requirement vary from month to month i.e., it should be between 3500 to 11,000 litre per day. Water is required more in May (11,000 litre/day) and is very low in November (3500 litre/day). Through drip the grape vine requires 40 to 50 cm of water. Through regular watering, if you consider the water requirement, only 50% is needed by drip method. If you follow the above method good buds can be expected and yield naturally will be good.

Drip and Fertilization:

In Karnataka at present the irrigation data shows that the watering through flood method is only 12.6%. In the near future the water application through drip is having lot of scope because in sugarcane through flooding the yield has come down by 50%. (Fig-22)

Grape Vine (6' x 4') drip/Ac/Day Water Requirement.

Month	Daily evaporation loss (mm)	Required water (litre/day/Ac)	Month daily evaporation loss (mm)	Daily evaporation loss mm	Required water litre /AC /day
April	11.05	7300	October	5.80	4000
May	11.82	10900	November	4.30	3500
June	8.93	8400	December	3.72	3400
July	5.85	6900	January	3.85	4000
August	4.85	5000	February	4.48	5700
Sept	4.82	5000	March	8.05	8300

(Dr. Subhash Shinde, Shetakari March 16)

Schedule of Drip Irrigation in grape Cultivation

Sl. No.	Days	Vine Management	Water requirement
	April		
1	Hard pruning (before 8 days) 7-14) days	-	Stop watering
2	15th April hard pruning	-	Stop watering
3	Days 16-30 April (15 days)	Sprouting	Take 0.6 yield factor and irrigation by drip
	May		
4	Days 1-15	Conopy spread 50 to 60	-
5	Days 16-31 (16 days)	Leaf growth 75-100 %	0.75% is yield factor taken and drip irrigation given.
	June to Sept		
6	Day 1 June to 30 Sept	Est. of flower primordia and maturity of cane	0.9 yield factor taken and drip irrigation given
	October		
7	Day 1 to 15 October pruning and previous 15 days.	-	Stop watering
8	15 October pruning	Keep buds and prune	-do-
9	Day 16 to 23 October (8days)	-	-do-
10	Day 24 October to 7 Nov (15 days)	Opening of buds and bunch sprouting	0.6 yield factor
	December		
11	Day 8 Nov to 27 Nov (25 days)	Fruit set completes and berry develops.	Take 0.8 yield factor and irrigate
12	Day 23 Dec to harvest	Filling of berry water	Take 0.90 yield factor and irrigate

Fertigation means what?

Method of fertilizer application through drip is called fertigation and following are the advantages of fertigation:

1) Fertilizers are applied to the nearest point of the roots and in equal proportion.
2) Fertilizer alongwith water are applied to the feeder roots.
3) As per the requirement the quantity and grade can be selected.
4) Fertigation reduces cost of labour, electricity and time. The insecticide and fungicides also can be mixed with fertigation to reduce labour cost. Soil structure is not hampered.
5) By fertigation 25% fertilizer can be saved. In that condition pH is 4.5, except in case of multi-K- which is having a pH of 9.5. They are acidic fertilizers and good for sodic, alkaline and calcareous soils. By fertigation more utilization of fertilizer is possible and they won't go beyond root hairs.

Type of Fertilizers Applied Through Drip:

1) **Liquid Fertilizers:** They fully get dissolved in water with low concentration and required in large quantity. Hence more transportation cost.

2) **Solid Soluble Fertilizers:**

They fully and easily dissolve in water and required in less quantity. Therefore it results in less transport cost and also it occupies less area. Soluble liquid and solid form of fertilizers are pure and pH will be 4.5 to 5.5 which helps in reducing soil pH. They should be dissolved in water in proportion of 1:10 or 1:15. One has to take care while going in for fertilizer application. Checking the drippers and fix-up of filters. They should have 0.08 to 0.15 mm holes. If the fertilizer granules are bigger than 0.08 to 0.15 filter helps in retaining them. Hence the dripper holes wont clog. They are costly example.urea, SOP, potassium nitrate. monoammonium phosphate are suitable to use alongwith water (1:10 to 1:15) and they should be passed through a cloth.

Fertigation System: Fertilizer alongwith water through drip are applied under pressure.

1) Through ventury, fertilizer alongwith water gets dissolved and applied.
2) Here the fertilizers are dissolved in a tank and through pump it is pumped in the main valve of the drip.
3) Delivery/flow bypass Tank: Here where the water is coming and going out through two small pipes connected to the main line and between a choke valve is connected. One entry pipe is connected to the tank and continuously fertilizer gets dissolved in water.
4) Fertilizer management: Based on crop, soil type, stage wise the fertilizers are applied.

Care of Drip System While Fertigation:

1) Keep filter clean.
2) Fertigation pump and tank examination.
3) Every month clean the dripper.
4) Observe level of salt in dripper; whether they are clogged, so clean them with acid or chlorine. Check up the pressure also.

I- Fertigation During April Pruning				
Month	Stage	Every week/dosage		Per month dosage
March	Rest period	13:13:13	6½ kg	25 kg
April	From pruning to twelth leaf	10:36:10 + Urea	6¼ kg 1.5 kg	25 kg 6 kg
May	Establishment of flower primordial	13:13:13	6¼ kg	25 kg
June	Maturity of cane	5:15:30 + 0:0:51	12½ kg 6¼ kg	50 kg 25 kg

Total nitrogen, phosphorus and potash /Ac Nitrogen 17kg, phosphorus 23 kg, potash 37 kg.

II - Fertigation during October Pruning				
Month	Stage	Every week/dosage		Per month dosage
October	Pruning to flowering	13:13:13 + Urea	6 ¼ kg 4.5 kg	25 kg 18 kg
November	Flowering to girdling	13:13:13 + Urea	6 ¼ kg 3 kg	25 kg 12 kg
December	Girdling to berry development	5:15:30 + 0:0:51	6 ¼ kg 6¼ kg	50 kg 25 kg
Total NPK/AC	Nitrogen 23 kg	P_2O_5 14 kg	Potash 34 kg	-
Yearly NPK/AC	Nitrogen 40 kg	P_2O_5 37 kg	Potash 71 kg	-

Note:

1) As per soil testing change the schedule
2) Foliar spray should be in early hours or evening and use sticker
3) Alongwith foliar spray, fungicide can be mixed.
4) Because of any reason, if growth of vine or bunch stops then spray 14:14:14, 4 to 5g/litre of water 2 to 3 times every week.

Sl. No.	Spraying Time	Grade		Dosage
II- April Pruning				
1	3-6 weeks	6-7 leaf stage	1 Microsole	50 g/ÀC
2	4-5 weeks	7-8 leaf stage	1 Magnesium nitrate	500 g/Ac
3	507 weeks	8-10 leaf stage	2 Calcium nitrate	500 g/Ac
4	7-8 weeks	Before pinching	3 Microsole	100 g/Ac
5	8-10 weeks	After pinching	1 Magnesium nitrate	500/Ac
6	10-12 weeks	Cane maturity	2 Calcium nitrate	500 g/Ac
II- October Pruning				
1	3-4 weeks	Immature bunch of parrot colour	Microsole	50g/Ac
2	4-5 weeks	Greenish bunch	Magnesium nitrate	500g/Ac
3	5-7 weeks	Bunch development	Calcium nitrate	500 g/Ac
4	7-8 weeks	Before girdling	Microsole-B	100g/Ac
5	8-10 weeks	Berry of Jowar size	Microsole-B	100g/Ac
6	10-12 weeks	Berry of pea size	Microsole-B	100g/Ac

Nutrient needs at different stages of growth

Sr. No.	Stage and days after pruning	Relative need		
		N	P	K
A.	**After Back Pruning**			
i.	Shoot growth period (1-30 days)	High	Medium	Nil
ii.	Fruit bud differentiation (31-60 days)	Low	High	Low
iii.	Fruit bud development (61-120 days)	Nil	Medium	High
iv.	Cane maturity (91-120 days)	Nil	Nil	Nil
B.	**After forward Pruning:**			
i.	Shoot growth period (1-40 days)	High	Low	Low
ii.	Flowering and berry set (41-70 days)	Medium	Medium	Medium
iii.	Berry growth (71-110 days)	Low	Low	High
iv.	Berry ripening (111-140 days)	Nil	Nil	Medium
C.	**After Harvest:**			
i.	Rest Period (1-15 days)	Low	Low	Low

2. Fertigation Schedule

Sr. No.	Stage	Formulation	Dose (Kg/ha/ day)	Nutrients (kg/ha/day)		
				N	P_2O_5	K_2O
A.	**After Back Pruning**					
	1-30 days	20-10-10	1.5	9.0	4.5	4.5
		Urea	1.0	13.8	0.0	0.0
	31-60 days	12-16-0	2.5	9.0	45.8	0.0
	61-90 days	0-0-51	2.5	0.0	0.0	46.0
	91-120 days	13-0-46	2.0	7.8	0.0	13.8
				39.6	50.3	64.3
B.	**After Forward Pruning**					
	1-40 days	19-19-19	2.0	15.2	15.2	15.2
		Urea	1.5	27.6	0.0	0.0
	41-70 days	12-61-0	1.0	3.6	18.3	0.0
		0-52-34	1.0	0.0	15.6	10.2
	71-110 days	13-0-46	2.0	10.4	0.0	36.8
		0-0-51	2.0	0.0	0.0	40.8
	111-130 days	0-0-51	3.0	0.0	0.0	30.6
				56.8	49.1	133.6
C.	**After Harvest**					
	1-15 days	19-19-19		2.9	2.9	2.9
	Total			**99.3**	**102.3**	**200.8**

1. Required doses of fertilizers in grapes:

		N	P_2O_5	K_2O
1.	Required nutrients (kg/ha)	300	500	1000
2.	Through organics (40%)	120	200	400
3.	Through inorganic nutrients in soil (30%)	090	150	300
4.	Through fertigation (20% equivalent to 30%)	90	100	200

Manurial Schedule:

A. Organics (200-200-400)

Source	**April-June**				**October-December**			
	Dose	**N**	**P_2O_5**	**K_2O**	**Dose**	**N**	**P_2O_5**	**K_2O**
FYM	30 t	75	30	180	30 t	75	30	180
Bone meal	1 t	10	120	-	-	-	-	-
Oil cake	-	-	-	-	1.5 t	30	15	45
Total		85	150	180		105	45	225

B. Inorganics (150-150-300)

Source	April-June (60-75-100)				October-December (90-75-200)			
	Dose	N	P_2O_5	K_2O	Dose	N	P_2O_5	K_2O
Super Phosphate	250	0	40	0	250	0	40	0
DAP	75	13.5	34.5	0	-	-	-	-
Urea	100	46	0	0	120	55	0	0
28-28-0	-	-	-	-	125	35	35	0
SOP	200	0	0	102	400	0	0	204
Total		59.5	74.5	102		90	75	204

Chapter 9

Use of Hormones in Grape Cultivation

By using Hormone:

1) Grape yield can be increased
2) Grape quality can be improved
3) Grape keeping quality and storage life can be increased

Different Hormones:-

1) Ethrel
2) GA (Gibberlic acid)
3) CCC (Lihocin)
4) NAA (Planofix)
5) Brassinosteoride (Combine)
6) 2-Chloro-4 Pyridil-N- Phenyl Urea (cppu)
7) 6 BA (Kinin)

While Using Hormone Understand the following:

1) Understand grape bunch establishment
2) Quality hormone should be used
3) Understand the effect of hormones
4) Use correct dosage of hormone

For Grape Production Use of Hormones:

Entire world uses hormones for getting higher yield in grape. In Thompson seedless unless we use hormones optimum grape production is not possible. After understanding it the use of hormones is begun. The yield is increased but quality is hampered and other problems may also be encountered. There will be chemical residue in fruits and after consumption it will affect the human body. Alongwith hormones the use of pesticide also affects the human health. In some places, after through examination in laboratory its results have revealed bad affliction on human health. Our grape consumers are increasing day-by-day and as also the European market is enlarging, there the consumers are worried about the effect of hormones on health.

On the one side the grape purchasers are rich and from the other side to fulfil the consumers desire, the responsibility lies on growers. Under such a situation, we have to search a way to use the hormones to increase the yield to meet the demand.

Grape Production and Different Types of Hormones:

At present almost all the grape growers use Gibberlic acid throughout the world. Chloromaquate, 4-CPA, 6BA, Ethrel, NAA, its usage helps in increasing the grape bunch size. The use of combine is also getting a momentum.

Crop Hormones Means what?

Crop hormone is a special type of organic chemical. It is effective and in a very short time the change can be observed with the food getting ready in a very short time mixed with crop hormones and growth regulators.

Types of Hormones:

Auxins, Gibberlins, Cytokinins, growth, retardants, and and Ethylene, likewise 5 types of hormones are used in grape cultivation.

Why to Use Hormones:

1) To maintain vigour of vine

2) To increase or decrease the berry length.

3) To get bunch colour

4) For longer shelf life.

5) To enhance the leaf life

6) In fruits, sugar, juice, acids, seeds and their quantity there is quality modification.

7) To enhance the development of berry

8) To delay in ripening

9) For defoliation.

All these qualities are affected by hormones which help in increasing the yield of grape.

When to use the hormones:

A) From April Pruning (hard pruning) to October Pruning: When the sprouts start growing, in order to initiate for proper food manufacturing, lot of money has to spent, then only the development of canes and the establishment of flower primordial takes place.

Secondly, when the canes are growing, the flower primordia starts moving towards the terminal end. Then the canes become barren. For growth of canes and branches either we have to increase or decrease the use of hormones like, CCC (Lihocin). They should be sprayed at 6-7 leaf stage, at 10-12 leaf stage and at 17-18 leaf stage. Likewise three times we have to use the hormones. Everytime taking into consideration the growth one has to decide the concentration of above said hormones. Everytime 500 ppm second time 700 ppm and third time 1000 ppm, is needed to be applied sometimes due to hard pruning; if water availability is a problem then the growth will be slow but in rainy season the growth will be fast. Under such situation only one spray of 1000 ppm CCC is advisable.

B) Establishment of flower primordia and hormonal requirement: In our climate after April pruning, within one to 1½ months the flower primordia establishment starts but after one and half month it will be slow. After 4-5 buds in front of canes for 100% flower primordia establishment we can use hormones.

For Perfect Establishment Use Uracil:

Uracil is one type of hormone which is used for flower primordia establishment. In our climate after April pruning when the new growth starts, the flower primordia establishment takes place and that period starts from 30-35 day after April pruning and it continues for another 30-35 days and as long as the growth continues the flowers primordia also emerges.

For Grape Productivity:

1) New sprout should be 30-35 days old for use of hormones.
2) This sprouting should have 6-10 buds.
3) Grape bud is a compound bud in which 2-3 buds comprises of leaf, tendril and bunch.

For our purpose 1 to 3 buds in new sprout of 30-35 days old is ideal with a compound bud. Once the primordia is established, it will last long and they develop and for that purpose uracil is required.

Use of Uracil:

1) Spray uracil on new growth when it attains 7-9 leaves; means total leaves of uniform area
2) Second; uracil spray on 10-12 leaves on branches.
3) Third; spray when the growth stops; means 16-20 leaves on branches.

   (This work should be completed before pinching of branches)

4) If we are going for sub-cane, then uracil spray should be taken up at 6-7 leaf stage. When you pinch the cane then 6 or 7 leaves develop. Third time application is carried out when the second pinching is done. One gram of uracil is mixed in 3 litres of water, then add 17 litres of water, totally 20 litres of water means it will be 40 ppm. For one acre, first spray requires about 150 litre and it requires 7.5 g uracil./Ac, For second spray 10 g uracil/Ac. means it is to be applied in 200 litres of water. For third spray, 250 litre of water is mixed with 12.5g of uracil. So totally for 3 sprays 600 litres of solution means 30 gram of uracil is necessary.

C) Establishment of flower Primordia and its period is important (cane maturity to development): There is a possibility of change in climate and so there is change in soil moisture, occurrence of pest and diseases which affect the establishment of flower primordia. If the sprouting is early or the growth is checked or the flower primordia melts, or the primordia moves towards terminal end then for better flower pirmordia, establishment of canes should be fully matured. For cane maturity C:N ratio should be optimum for leaf colour, size and their number which decides the size of flower primodia. Some time Anthracnose (Karapa) on quick growing branches affects the primordia than in axil, growth won't come under such situation. We have to see that the primordia is established by means of application 6 BA. This hormone contains Kinetin which can be dissolved in Ispropyl Alcohol with approx 5 ppm of two sprays are required. For one acre 2g and 6 BA is sufficient. Totally under favourable situation, lihocin uracil and 6 BA; two or three times it is sprayed for getting double yield.

D) Control of post-emergence aerial roots on vine:

Even though watering is done, it is not available for plants. under such situations aerial roots appear on plant body, main trunk or stem. More aerial roots affect the hormonal balance on the canes, on buds hairy growth appears which increases the bud dormancy. In this condition after October pruning, the bud burst will be delayed, even application of Dormex becomes useless for that purpose. Before October pruning NAA of 20 ppm is recommended or per Ac 100 ml Plano-fix in 200-225 liter of water is sprayed. When there are no aerial roots before October pruning these sprays should be taken with NAA application @ 20ppm 3-4 week as a foliar spray.

II) From October Pruning to Harvesting:

1) Before October pruning
2) While doing pruning – first step
3) After October pruning – second step
4) After October pruning – third step.

Before harvesting of grape: Take up 15 days before NAA-10 ppm or planofix spray which helps in reducing berry shattering/berry drop.

Other Hormonal Use:

1) Ethrel: For defoliation Ethrel @ of 1000 ppm to 2500 ppm is recommended. When pruning is to attended to without leaf removal then Ethrel is used after pruning for defoliation. Application of ethrel for defoliation results in accumulation of ethylene in vine but in coloured varieties like kishmish charani (sharad seedless), flame seedless, joyti seedless it results in colour development during ripening.

   Second time application of Ethrel is needed when the grape ripening starts and it helps in case of coloured varieties for proper and uniform colour development. To apply ethrel @ 500 ppm, 200 litres quantity per acre is required. When the coloured varieties are to be sent for early marketing and then for sugar development, ethrel is useful. For varieties like kishmish charni, flame seedless, muscat, gulabi, ethrel is useful. In market Ethrel is available in different names– Ethrel, Ethopan, Thril, florel, Sefa, Cinon. The chemical name is 2- Flora, Ethyl Phosphonic acid. It dissolves early in water and it is available in a concentration of 39%.

Ethrel 250 ml/100 liter of water – 1000 ppm

Ethrel 500 ml/100 of water – 2000 ppm

Ethrel 125 ml/100 liter of water – 500 ppm

Ethrel 625 ml/100 liter of water – 2500 ppm

2) Gibberlic acid:

Gibberlic acid is available to plants as Gibberlic which is helpful for cell elongation, bunch thinning, berry elongation and rachis elongation. After October pruning, bunch will be soft and at that time it is used. At the stages of small leaves and bunch of parrot colour, which turns to green colour, 10 ppm of GA has to be used on bunches which helps in elongation of bunch; at times 20 ppm GA has to be used for more than 20 ppm GA by which process the rachis, after elongation, turns upward or it leads to bending, or the bunch near the stalk breaks and falls down. The GA has to be used 25-30 days after October pruning, if used early then less results are expected. Gibberlic acid for second time has to be used before bunch flowering starts capfall. At this stage GA helps in elongation of berry stalk, swelling of berries and thinning helps in providing space for development of berries, thereby bunch will not be compact. All the berries should be uniform in size with excess shedding leads to loosenofbunch weight. For berry elongation, third time of GA spray is used. Within bunch to increase berry length and swelling, GA @ 25 to 40 ppm during 75 to 100% flowering is recommended. If less cane of GA is applied, the berries become round in shape.

The diameter and length of berries should be in 1:2 proportion. When 60-75% capfall-25 ppm, GA at 70-80% capfall-30 ppm, 80-90% capfall - 35 ppm, 90-100% capfall 40-

ppm, GA should be used.

How to prepare GA solution:

One gram of GA is dissolved in 50 ml. acetone and add it to one litre of water it will then be one litre of stock solution.

1) 1 gm GA + 1 litre stock solution + 99 litres of water = 100 litre = 10 ppm

20 1 g GA + 1 litre stock solution + 49 litres of water = 50 litre = 20 ppm

3) 1 g GA + 1 litre stock solution + 39 litres of water = 40 litre = 25ppm

4) 1 gm GA + 1 litre of stock solution + 19 litres of water = 20 litre = 50ppm

5) 1 gm GA + 2 litres of stock solution + 19 litre of water = 20 litre= 50 ppm

6) 1 gm GA + one litre stock solution + 9 litres of water = 10 litres = 100 ppm

7) 1 g GA + one litre stock solution-1000 ppm

3) Chloromaquate (Lithocin):

Chloromaquate, Cyocel, CCC and Lihocin are the synonyms available in the market. This is growth-retardant hormone and is widely used in grape cultivation. It is widely used, when rain occurs, new growth comes very fast and the growth in front of bunch will be very fast. In slow growth of the bunch, under such situation to check the growth, use of Lihocin is recommend. After October pruning when the bunch and bunch growth is soft Lihocin should be used. New growth at this stage is very fast with the availability of metabolite and continuously by growth with 5th and 6th bud bunch that comes out.

The very purpose of CCC is to divert the metabolites towards the bunch for proper growth by hindering the flow of sap towards the growing tip, which results in improvement of bunch growth.

How to use CCC

After October pruning, when 5th, 6th buds are soft that means when its colour is yellowish or parrot colour CCC is sprayed because growth conditions are not same on all bunch of vines and when CCC is used at new growing points, growth gets slowed down and bunch develops. Food manufacturing power of leaves increases. When the metabolites move towards growing points it stops, the manufacturing power of new leaf increases this way and the metabolites moves towards the bunch in double quantity.

How much to Use CCC:

If used at proper time then 250 ppm is sufficient. Initially low dosage of 200 ppm, two days before 125 ppm, this process is delayed, then 375 to 450 ppm of third spray is required. However more than 500 ppm of foliar spray is harmful.

How to Prepare CCC:

This is available at 50% concentration, which is easily dissolved in water. Method of preparation of 100 litres of different concentration of CCC is as given below:

1) 100 ml Lihocon + 100 liters of water = 500 ppm
2) 50 ml Lihocon + 100 liters of water = 250 ppm
3) 40 ml Lihocon + 100 liters of water = 200 ppm
4) 75 ml Lihocon + 100 liters of water = 375 ppm
5) 60 ml Lihocon + 100 liters of water = 300 ppm
6) 90 ml Lihocon + 100 liters of water = 450 ppm

Precaution While Using CCC:

1) While using CCC the soil should be wet.

2) While doing foliar spray, from leaves to growing point, from bunch to growing tip-the spraying is recommended.

3) On sprout when 6-7 leaves are available and later when 5-6 leaves are there, it is more effective.

4) If Anthracnose is expected then mix carbendizim alongwith fungicide and spray.

5) If flea beetle is observed then mix insecticide alongwith Lihocin and spray.

Note:

1) If irrigation and Nitrogen are more, then control of disease and pest and will be difficult so after two days a second time spray.

2) If by mistake higher dosage is used, then in near future it will have bad effect.

3) Apply immediately 25 kg urea and irrigate fully.

4) Immediately 200 gm urea in 100 litres of water is to be mixed and take up foliar spray.

5) Take 10 ppm GA foliar spray.

4) 6BA:

This comes under Kinetin or Kinin group and almost all farmers are using 6 BA. It is used for cell division, which further leads to berry development. Leaf is required for food manufacturing. It helps in increasing bunch weight and development of sugars. As soon as the girdling is over, 6 BA @ 5 to 7 ppm has to be sprayed. After GA spray if girdling is delayed then 6BA be sprayed. If the girdling effect is not visible immediately, then 10-12 ppm 6 BA spray is required.

Application of 6 BA's are needed in two sprays. First 20 ppm and second one < 20 ppm. 6 BA has to be dissolved in isoproply alcohol or in ammonium chloride. For berry elongation if GA application is delayed then the GA 10 ppm + 6 BA 10 ppm can also be taken as foliar spray.

1) For berry elongation, within 3-4 days, GA 40 ppm + 6BA 4 ppm is needed when bunch is nipped at bottom.

2) 8-10 ppm 6 BA spray on leaf and bunch.

5) NAA (Planofix):

Naphthalene acetic acid is utilized for specific purpose to prevent bunch drop or to stop small bunch melting with 20 ppm NAA 3 spray. At fruit set NAA application helps in getting good natural bloom. Before harvest to reduce the berry drop, you can prolong the harvest period for a week. 100 ml of Plano fix per acre is sufficient. If the crop load is optimum then other hormones are used in equal concentration then the Plano fix spray is not necessary. If you are expecting > 12.5 tones/Ac then NAA application for proper yield is useful.

6) Combine: (Brassinosteoride):

It is a Brassinosteoride based hormone. It helps in cell elongation and cell division at quicker rate. It also helps to stand the adverse climatic situation.

1) Grape berry development.

2) It helps in grape pedicel thickness, so it helps in reduction of pre and post berry drop.

3) Berry and bunch weight increases.

4) Grape storage life enhances, keeping quality improvement during transit.

5) Uniform grape quality helps in export.

How to use combine:

It should be used alongwith Gibberlic acid. It has to be used when berries have set. After fruit set the GA and combine should be in equal proportion, then again repeat and you will get good results. So 2-3 mixed spray of GA and combine are required.

Combine+GA ratio for Foliar Spray:

1) At fruit set (before bajra-size berry) combine 100 milli + 3 g GA = 100 litre of water = 30 ppm

2) One week after dipping, second dipping has to be done. At this stage combine 100 milli + 4g GA = 100 litres of water (40 ppm) or after first dipping with 10 days gap combine 100 mill + 5 g GA = 100 liter of water (50 ppm)

Note:

1) In a combine, GA totally dissolves, so dissolving GA in acetone is not necessary.

2) In readymade solution (sticking agent) for every 100 litres, apply 25 milli apsa -80 or any sticker.

6. CPPU

CPPU helps in cell elongation. It also helps in speeding the process of increase in berry diameter. CPPU along with GA or alone can be used. CPPU is used at a concentration of 1 to 2 ppm. If used at more than 2 ppm then the shape of berry gets spoilt and also there will be cracking, CPPU if used at early stage, will have effect on colour in the later stage. CPPU is used between fruit and a 10 mm berry size and used 3-4 times because during the period GA is used 2-3 times.

How much to be used/acre:

1) CCC: 250 ppm/Ac 150 to 200 litres means 250 milli Lihocin in 200 liters of water or CCC 250 milli or chloromaquate ml in 200 litres.

CPPU + GA Dosage for Use

Name of Hormone	Bunch size/Size of berry/dosage				
	4 mm	6 mm	8 mm	10 mm	Total
GA	30 ppm	40 ppm	50 ppm	60 ppm	180
CPPU	2 ppm	2 ppm	2 ppm	2 ppm	8
GA	10 ppm	50 ppm	50 ppm	50 ppm	160
CPPU	1.5 ppm	2 ppm	2.5 ppm	3 ppm	9
GA	35 ppm	40 ppm	50 ppm	50 ppm	170
CPPU	2.0 ppm	2 ppm	2 ppm	-	6

Or 5 ppm CPPU, 30 to 40 ppm GA together can be used. At present CPPU 0.1% conc. solution is available, for that the following schedule is to be followed:

0.1 % CPPU Solution	Already prepared GA	CPPU (ppm) Milli
100	100 litre	1
200	100 litre	2
300	100 litre	3
400	100 litre	4
500	100 litre	5

Use of Hormone

Sl. No	After October Pruning	Bunch stage, leaf stage	Conc of hormone
1	Approximately 3 weeks	6-7 leaves bunch, parrot colour	CCC 200 to 250 ppm
2	Approximately 4 weeks	Before bunch development	GA 15 to 20 ppm

Sl. No	After October Pruning	Bunch stages leaf stage	Conc of hormone
3	Approximate 5 weeks	Bunch development	GA 20 to 25 ppm
4	Approximate 6 weeks	Bunch development	GA 25 to 30 ppm + 6 BA 5-10 ppm
5	Approximate 7 weeks	Full bunch development	GA 25 to 30 ppm + combine
6	Approximate 8 weeks	Full fruit set	GA 40 to 50 ppm + combine
7	Approximate 12 weeks	Bunch ripening	NAA 10-20 ppm
8	Approximate 14 weeks	2-3 weeks before harvest	15 to 25 ppm NAA

Sl. No.	Bunch Stage	Name of hormone	Conce of hormones
1	Early pre-bloom	Lihocin/CCC	200 to 250 ppm
2	Pre-bloom	Gibberlic acid	10-15 ppm
3	Pre-bloom	Gibberlic acid	15-20 ppm
4	50 % flowering	GA + 6 BA	20 TO 25 ppm + 2 to 2.5 ppm
5	75 % flowering	GA + 6 BA	25 to 30 ppm + 2.0 to 2.5 ppm
6	Immediately after fruit set	Gibberlic acid + combine	30 to 40 ppm
7	Berry of jowar grain size	GA + combine	40 to 50 ppm

Main purpose of Growth Regulators:

At the present situation for export of grape good production is the main aim. On an average 12 tonnes per acre is easily expected, but 15 tonnes per acre is required. In grape, the quality means the length, TSS, colour and these three aspects are very important.

The berry shape means length and diameter should be same or they should be in equal proportion. A berry diameter of 18 mm and a length of 24 mm is possible by using growth regulator and alongwith that a sugar percentage of 20 is necessary. Once the bunch is ready in white varieties it will be milky/greenish but in coloured varieties the colour should be dark and uniform. Alongwith that the climate, the vine care, the bunch load, nutrition–all these points one has to take into consideration.

Approximately 3 weeks after October pruning one has to understand the bunch situation and while using hormone the sticker Apsa-80 25ml/100 litres will give good results of the hormone effects.

Chapter 10

Girdling and Thinning

- For taking grapes to good production alongwith growth regulators, girdling and thinning are also necessary.
- For girdling and thinning there is no alternative. Girdling should be done in time and in a proper way. The injury caused by girdling should heal in time.
- Thinning should be carried out every week.
- Between bunch thinning, bunch tipping, berry thinning and flower thinning, there is distinct difference, therefore, proper care of bunch and leaf is very important. For bunch tipping, how many leaves to be maintained after fruit set and whether leaf has to be kept then encouraging the bunching, take care of all these points will make difficult work easy.

Girdling:

To increase the sugar development in grape bunch and to increase the bunch weight, girlding is done. Girdling is done after GA is used. Girdling helps in increasing the yield by 1.5 to 2 times, that is why girdling is a must.

Girdling Means What?

On any part of a grapevine if a circular cut is given it is called girdling. This is done on canes, on T's (main arm) and on main stem (trunk). Cane girdling have lots of benefit but by running girdling on vine many bunch will have positive effect and from trunk girdling all the bunch will get the benefit.

1) Cane girdling has to be done on every bunch and it

requires a lot of time, lot of labour and a lot of money. On an average girdling of 40,000 canes is required.

2) Arm girdling is done on the canopy. On every vine 2 to 4 T are there and on an average 3000 arms are there in an acre. Arms (T) are at a two meter height, the girdling will be very cumbersome and also using of girdling plier is not easy; ultimately the labours are not happy with this kind of girdling.

3) Trunk girdling is done very easily with an average closer spacing if about 1800 vines are available so by engaging more labour in 4-5 days this work can be completed in time. In a wider spacing again it will be very easy. But, in all bunches equal balance is not available.

When Girdling has to be Done:

The objective of girdling is to improve yield quality. Immediately after October pruning, once fruit is set, girdling is done. If this process is done in a hurry or early the purpose is not served. After girdling, the food manufactured in leaves definitely goes to branches and will be available to bunches. Before girdling tipping sprouts are a must. The food which is not moving towards bunches will move towards the terminal growth. The vigorous growth affects the bunch growth. When the grapes are at flowering stage the vine nutrition availability will be limiting; naturally the demand for food/nutrition increases. In seedless grape varieties, at fruit set stage the GA and other growth regulators, if already applied and girdling is done, will have very good effect.

If girdling is done early the fruit set percentage increases and the bunch will be too compact. Within a bunch for formation of the berries every berry development space availability is difficult hence may result in berry gettting flattened and finally the berry length reduces and the diameter increases. If this process is reversed then the weight of the bunch and one % sugar also reduces and the quality of berries at distal and proximal deteriorates.

At present situation if early girdling has to be done then do it on trunk and if late then do it on canopy area. In our place the height of the trunk is 1.5 to 2 meters and the girdling at 25 cm above ground has to be avoided. When soil is raised and water comes in contact with the girdling zone, then the fungus moves in plants through injury. If watering is done by drip then it is excellent and very important.

In a normal situation the centre of the trunk girdling is advised. Girdling at a height is cumbersome. At the time of girdling near the bunch if the distance is more, then girdling results get delayed. After October pruning if the gridling is done at 6th bud and the same if you do at 10th bud then the results are encouraging. In 4-arm kniffin system the lower arm shows good results than the upper arms. While doing girdling another point one has to keep in mind is that the total bunches on vine, total number of branches and sterile branches should have optimum leaves. If more bunches are there, then the result is late. If the total number of bunches, the sprouting and leaves are more then the result will be late and but it will be very good.

Care While Doing Girdling:

Irrigation of land: While girdling operation is on there should be sufficient water in the soil. If the soil is dry then barks come out easily. Too much wetting of land is not advisable since the healing process is not uniform and leaves get yellowish. If formation of other leaves actively slow down then the girdling effect is not visible. For good results the soil should be wet.

Bunch care: Once the fruit sets in and bunch tipping is completed then girdling is advised. Around 70-80 % of bunch setting is necessary to go for girdling, girdling should also be completed in the same day.

Application of Fungicide on Girdling Places:

If girdling is done closer to ground and the soil is too wet then application of fungicide becomes necessary because the injury caused by girdling provides place to enter the fungus. Dead arm, Botrydiplodia, mealy bug, stems borer may create problems. Usually attention is given towards care of pests and diseases but not towards the trunk. Therefore, before the disease/insect are noticed, spraying of chemicals viz Blitox, Captaf, Ziride, Dithane-M-45, Bavistin, Nuvan, Carbaryl. Malathion etc., and mixture pasting is necessary and this work should be completed on the same day of girdling.

Proper Time Injury Healing of Girdling:

Girdling in time and in a proper way should be done and callus formation within 15 days takes place and in another one week the injury healing takes places. Deep girlding not only takes more time for healing but inside it will be hollow. Girdling nearer to ground heals late than the girdling which is nearer to canopy. Under such situation it means during favourable situation utmost care of bunch is necessary and before girdling apply hormonal paste. For callus formation apply Indole acetic acid or Indole Butryic acid (IAA/IBA) of 1000 ppm. On the surface of girdling injury, cows compost + urine helps in healing of injury. Through compost and urine we cannot control insects/diseases, the callus formation starts from top of the surrounding but the fungus starts from below the injury nearer to ground. Therefore fungicide/hormone should be applied to these particular places. In cow compost CoC, Nuvan, mixing is economical. For one kg compost mix 25g fungicide + 20g/milli insecticide and paste it. On the emergence of new leaves the sap flow starts through the trunk. For initiation of new growth we have to go for application of fertilizer. New leaves which are dark green in colour and full in size are capable of manufacturing food and for their maintenance, nutrient management is necessary. At least 15 days time is required for maturity and within 40-45 days, photosynthesis capacity exists which means 55 to 60 days after

October pruning; the photosynthesis activity will be maximum then it gets slowed down. For taking this benefit girdling has to be done within 60 days of pruning. On vine, active photosynthesis in leaves continues for 42 days whose benefit we have to harvest,. The new sprout, when it is soft, the carbohydrate (food) moves towards the terminal end then it moves down to trunk then again through branches moves towards bunch. This natural process sometimes gets delayed but to start early in time girdling is necessary.

During girdling, growth will not stop and the sap will not move towards the bunch but it moves towards the terminal portion and girdling effect will not be observed. Before fruit set it means during bunch emergence the growth checks and girdling process will have to be completed then fruit set increases within the bunch which will be too compact. Fruit set is easy and comes to harvest early also. At the time when the bunch gets ready early then bunch weight will not be much and also sugar % less. In a bunch if the setting is not uniform and girdling is over the berries get the benefit of girdling. The benefit on an average is noticed before girdling if bunch thinning and tipping is attended to.

When the grape bunch starts developing after girdling the bunch quality can be improved. Within a vine, if more number of bunches are there or if more fruit setting in a bunch is observed, then bunch development has to be restricted which further delays sugar development and in order to overcome these two problems girdling helps because bunch and leaves number may not increase. The girdling effect is visible within a week. After girdling increases in fruit weight and quality cane is observed then necessary fertilizers and hormonal use can be avoided.

Thinning:

In a grape all the berries within a bunch, all the bunches within the vine and all the vines within a garden should be uniform and for the purpose of export, thinning is very important.

Thinning means What?

The common meaning of thinning is some excess berries from a bunch are removed and counted number of berries in a bunch we have to keep. For every thinning operation we have to see how many bunch per vine are there and what should be the leaf area for every bunch; all these points should be kept in mind and then only we should do the thinning.

Types of thinning:

Following are the types of thinning:

1) Leaf thinning
2) Bunch thinning

A) Leaf thinning:

1) Tipping of sprouts
2) Removing of leaves from branches
3) Removing of branches.

B) Bunch thinning:

1) Removal of few full bunches
2) Pinching of bunch
3) Berry thinning

While doing thinning, leaf or bunch thinning one has to attend:

When Thinning is done?

For getting quality bunch once the bunch emerges on vine and fruit setting is complete then bunch are counted, immediately thinning work starts for getting good result. After fruit formation the thinning is not beneficial, rather it is harmful.

When leaf and bunch thinning starts, don't apply any nutrition or hormones manually but to stop the entry of disease/insects both fungicide/insecticides can be used.

1) Removal of Excess Growth:

After October pruning there are two types of growth one grows alongwith bunch secondly another grows without bunch. This growth should be removed immediately at the beginning stage itself, otherwise the supply of nutrient of bunch will be less which results in weak bunch.

While October pruning is in operation, if you keep more canes and more number of buds (10) per cane or pruning is done by keeping more canes on vine or early pruning is done, then more vegetative growth is observed, the growth of which have to be removed as early as possible. Usually in a cane, at terminal 3-4 buds position, more growth is observed. On vine the fruit (bunch) load is at 5-7 buds, excess growth at tips is removed after October pruning to stop new growth and at the bottom of 3-4 buds apply Bordeaux paste.

2) Tipping of bunches:

The bunches at the tip are sour and small in size. Only the long bunches are not advisable for packing in boxes. For this purpose by thinning you have to give a good shape to the bunches. For tipping of bunch use scissors only and do thinning with 10% tipping which is a must and maximum up to 30% bunch tipping is advisable.

In grape bunch after fruit set, the berry nutrition management and its growth starts very fast. New leaves expansion completes and food manufacturing starts. On vine every bunch and berries of bunch, balanced nutrition is the responsibility of leaves on the vine. The food manufactured by leaves goes to leaves, and some will go for the emergence of the new leaves and some portion of the food goes to branches, roots, bunches etc. If the food availability in plant is less than the actual vegetative growth is observed. Then the branches will be longer and to stop this growth we have to pinch it only by means that can save the food. Alongwith this girdling it also helps in storing the food by leaves and will be utilized by the bunches. Girdling checks the flow of sap to roots and bigger portion goes to the bunches. There it helps in improving the bunch size and berry size. Checking of branch growth should be done earlier.

This process on vine improves food manufacturing capacity in the leaves and in other words girdling is a checkpost to stop the downward flow of nutrients that helps the bunch to develop. Excess removal of growth makes the vine empty. Then sometimes stopping of growth is not possible under such situation; excess vegetative growth should not be stopped immediately; their growth has to be stopped at 6-7 leaves which helps in food manufacturing.

Sometimes the growth with or without bunch will be stunted or immediately they become stunted and after pinching we won't get the required leaves, the leaves become smaller in size. Under such situation before pinching, girdling should be done first. On vine some branches are vigorous and some are stunted. Hence in the vigorously growing branches pinching is done to stop the growth then immediately girdling should be attended to. For the growth of the terminal end, girdling should be done with utmost care and for that purpose, for single girdling one acre is advocated and within 4-6 days callus formation and further flow of sap should take place.

Second important point is after thinning, looking to the number of branches the number of berries per bunch, you have to increase the number of leaves. For increasing the yield and more number of bunches for good quality, less number of bunches are required. If you are not keeping equal proportion of bunches and leaves then the number of bunches will be more in vine.

Proper number of bunches per hectare or acre are to be taken into consideration and how many bunches per vine are there, how many canes on a vine and on each cane how many bunches and number of leaves are there all these we have to keep in mind.

For example on one cane ½ kg bunch should have 150 berries and that cane should have 15 leaves; that means for one leaf 10 berries are required. The leaves behind the bunch should be 6 and in the bunch 9 leaves, so totally 15 leaves are necessary.

In Thompson Seedless more than 500 berries will be there per bunch. For retention after flower thinning, 30 % thinning of berries or tipping of bunch, 30 % thinning or so from the total number of berries, approximately 1/3 berries we have to keep for optimum berry production. After a week the tipping is done, keep required number of leaves so as to have good aeration.

For bunch nutrition the food comes from leaves but whatever the food manufactured it won't go to leaves but to fulfil the vine nutrition requirement it goes to different parts. On vine sometimes branches without bunch growth will be there and by keeping 6-7 leaves tipping is done for utilization of manufactured food by vines.

Chapter 11

Pest and Disease Control

1) Quality grape production and export.
2) Keep an eye on important disease and their symptoms.
3) Keep an eye on harmful insects.
4) At what stage which disease and what insect-strike.
5) Suitable climate means what precautionary measures one has to take.
6) Take prophylectic measures than curative ones. After the treatment, 100% control is not possible. Therefore take control measures and timely control of pest and diseases is very important.

In-time crop care:

Whatever variety of grape you grow it should be free from pests and diseases. Countries may not purchase disease-affected grapes. In Karnataka to get disease-free grape cultivation, it is a towering task and a costly affair in which only in case of ripened grape condition you won't find the pest and disease. In our place the climate is often changing. As soon as the October rain stops and flower emerges there is severe cold temperature which the bunch has to tolerate and in a very severe hot temperature the fruit ripens. In the last 8-10 years situation, you will see timely flowering till harvest. Sometimes, cold temperature, fog, cyclonic rains and hailstorm damages grape cultivation.

Such situation may not arise at once but sometimes insect and disease problem may arise, while sometimes it may go simultaneously. After October pruning the crop requires

120 days for harvest.

Four-point disease-free programme:

1) Good sanitation.
2) Use of standard fungicide and insecticide.
3) A comprehensive pest and disease control programme.
4) Nutrition management.

Maintaining a clean garden:

At the time of October pruning keep the garden clean, particularly the disease-affected leaves which may be collected and burnt before actual October pruning.

Before October pruning the insect-affected branches are cut but disease-affected leaves are left as it is on the vine. These leaves are removed during October pruning. On such leaves powdery mildew, downy mildew, Botrytis, anthracnose infection may affect plants as well as soil, and immediately on newly emerged leaves, before October pruning one may notice anthracnose. Therefore, all these leaves may be collected and burnt outside the garden.

2) A Comprehensive Pest and Disease Control Programme:

Immediately after October pruning, anthracnose will be noticed on newly emerging, soft and succulent branches along with flea beetle. To control this after October pruning apply bordeaux paste and water soluble. Carbaryl dust, Cofidor 0.3 ml/liter may be applied in the garden.

On vines when there is new sprout and bunch emergence, keep application of fungicide/insecticide on new leaves continuously. Till the berries attain a pea size, pest and disease problem will be severe. Under such situation keep an eye on the climate and analyse the possibility of disease which may be identified and take immediate control measures. Climate means temperature, humidity, precipitation, (Fog, rainfall) etc.

There is a co-relation between temperature, humidity and diseases. Understand the following:

Sl. No.	Stage	Period	Climate	Disease/ insect possibility
1	October pruning and emergence of new sprout.	October	Hot and humid climate with rains.	Anthracnose, Flea beetle
2	New bunch, new sprouts, bunch flowering, insects.	November	Cold climate, fog, cloudy weather	Downy mildew, Anthracnose.
3	Fruit set leaves and cane growth, bunch growth, berry development	December	Severe cold wave clouds, hailstorm	Anthracnose and powdery mildew, DM Lepidopteron insects
4	Berry development stops, ripening starts, then Harvesting	January February	Cold air hailstorm fluctuatio n of temperat ure	Berry drop mealy bug, bunch berry drop.

It means after October pruning two months are very crucial, very delicate and an equally dangerous period.

Sl. No.	Disease	Temperature	Relative humidity (%)
1	Anthracnose	30-32°C	60-100 %
2	Downy mildew	12-14°C	60-90 %
3	Powdery mildew	20-24°C	40-90 %
4	Phomopsis	23-26°C	90-100 %
5	Diplodia	25-30°C	80-100 %

In our place the minimum temperature during November and December will be between 12-20°C whereas the maximum temperature is noticed between 24-32°C. In the atmosphere the relative humidity is 50-75 %. After watering orchard and following rainfall and mist, the spraying percentage may increase. The above diseases may spread if there is no proper phytosanitation. Temperature and RH go hand in hand and such situation is most congenial for disease spread. If temperature or RH, is increasing then take up foliar spray of fungicide. During this period give foliar spray or dusting of cane. When RH increases then take up dusting. If foliar spray is difficult, the quantity required per hectare is less then use good nozzle pump. The per hectare water requirement is 500 lit. If it is more than 500 lit. then RH increases. When the fungicide spray does not fall on the leaves, there will be fungal infection which will be very quick. While taking up fungicide foliar spray one has to keep in mind that foliar spray should reach young sprout tips, leaves and bunches. For that excess leaves should be removed. Tie the canes to the wire for proper spray, so that the leaves can harvest sunrays and good air.

Benefits of disease control:

By keeping orchard clean, the possibility of disease occurrence gets very much reduced. If you don't do it then immediately you will find the diseases on leaves and bunches. If such a situation arises, then immediately take control measures. For this purpose you have to identify the diseases and decide which chemicals you have to spray. If control is not possible with one spray then repeat the spray but change the chemical. For control of one disease there are several chemicals available, in which contact and systemic types are available. Use both of them.

Disease controlling Fungicides

Sl. No.	Diseases	Contact Fungicides	Systemic fungicides
1	Anthracnose (Karpa)	1) Bordeaux mixture 2) Copper oxy chloride	1) Benlate 2) Bavistin 3) Topsin-M 4) Score 5) Bayeor
2	Dowmy mildew	1) Bordeaux mixture 2) Copper oxy chloride 3) Phytolexin-84	1) Ridomil 2) Metalyxil 3) Alliette 4) Curzat
3	Powdry mildew (Buri)	1) Wet. Sulf 2) Mycosole	1) Beletan 2) Rubigan 3) Contof
4	Phomopsis	1) Bordeaux mixture 2) Captan	1) Quintal 2) Benomyl
5	Diplodia	1) Bordeaux mixture 2) Copper oxy chloride	1) Benomyl
6	Bacterial blight (Xanthomonas)	1) Ziram (3) CoC 2) Captan	1) Benlate

Note: To understand trade name, common name or chemical name details are given (Package of practice list to be included)

3) Nutrition Management:

In grape garden, if nutrition management is not proper, then the disease problem may increase in gardens where nitrogen application is more and the diseases increase because excess nitrogen may bring more sprouting which are prone to anthracnose disease.

In places where magnesium deficiency is observed, in such gardens downy mildew disease may cause more damage. Application of potash brings resistance against diseases not only in grape but in other crop also. We can conclude in this way, excess and unnecessary application of nitrogen should be avoided. Magnesium and potash use helps in overcoming many diseases. If the disease resistance increases in plants then disease control may become easy.

Overall care:

After October pruning, in 79-90 days, the ripening starts, in another 30 days the harvesting gets completed. During 75-90 days the disease may cause partial or total damage. In this period four important points (cleanliness, healthy leaves, controlling disease, foliar spray) may totally help in control of diseases. After this period stop spraying of any fungicide.

While taking up quality grape production cleanliness go for, exact control measures and healthy leaves –the three factors decide and controls 75% disease and 25% disease can be taken care. If initially not controlled it may increase, which may reflect on the quality of the fruits and leaves. The fruit bunches are the most affected ones.

October Post-Pruning Diseases and Control Measures:

After October Pruning, new sprouts and disease emerges simultaneously.

1) Very soft growth or bunch - Anthracnose
2) Fruit set - Downy Mildew
3) Bunch development - Xanthomonas
4) Berry development - Powdery Mildew
5) Berry development - Botrytis
6) Berry ripening - Botrytis

Major disease symptoms:

1) Downy Mildew:

Initially on leaves small sized light-greenish with yellow spots are observed on leaves. In a very short time in a humid climate on lower side of the leaves spores develop, then that part will become whitish in colour. Later on white patches light yellowish colour develops. Then slowly the diameter of patches increases but in severe cases the leaves may fall. Apart from leaves the young sprouts also show whitish patch, then the growth stops or the affected sprout gets dried or the leaves may fall.

Control measure:

Downy Mildew (*Plasmopora Viticola*) is a fungus. The disease initially spreads by spores on vines by turn. The left over inoculum on light green leaves may act as a source in bunches of wine while the spores may germinate in congenial condition and these spores on newly emerged shoots get rooted. If the quantum of rain is more, then the disease may spread very rapidly. The atmosphere, relative humidity up to 85% and more, if persists, plays an important role, in atmospheric temperature. If the temperature is prevailing between 10° to 30°C, then only the disease may increase or decrease. But 90-100 % of relative humidity with 24°C to 26°C temperature, the spread of the disease will be very fast.

Timely Disease Control:

1)	After October pruning, when new growth starts:	Carbendizim
2)	After 12-15 days	Carbendizim
3)	After 4-5 days	Ridomil
4)	After 12-15 days	Ridomil
5)	3-4 days	Streptocyclin
6)	8-10 days	Beletan
7)	8-10 days	Microsule
8)	8-10 days	Beletan/Rubigan
9)	10-12 days	Benlate/Benomyl
10	10-12 days	Benlate/Benomyl
Totally in 85 to 95 days		Take up 10 spray

2) Anthracnose (*Gloeosporium* ampelophagum) (Karpa)

First symptoms will appear on soft shoot and young leaves. On leaves around 5 mm diameter spots are visible or thick spots reddish in colour, at later stage the centre of the spots becomes brownish in colour and that centre position may dry and fall off. The young leaves are the first victims of the disease. The sunken spots on canes are observed the during rainy season. The disease is also noticed on petioles with high relative humidity causing red spots on the diseased spot.

Control measures:

Congenial atmosphere is most suitable for its spread, because the mycelium may remain on the canes after the pruning, and when the rain starts within 24 hours mycelium starts developing, then they enter the leaves and the symptoms start appearing for which 32°C for 4 days is sufficient alongwith the rains. Relative humidity (90%) which are most suitable for its spread may result in a major setback to farmers or loss.

3) Powdry mildew: (Buri) (*Uncinula necator*)

On every soft and green vine the affected portion may become whitish in colour. Later the colour may change to brownish. The margin shows more infection; when the infection increases it spreads on entire leaves; at later stages the powdery growth on both lower and upper region is observed. If the climate is cold the margin may dry up. On the tip of new sprouts you will find powdery growth. At flower primordia stage, powdery mildew infection may cause more damage.

Control measure:

Uncinula necator is a fungus on vine greenish portion and it affects most of the fungal mycelium and spores and one season to anther season they persist on vines and canes. Already infected buds sprouts in a suitable climate, therefore, spread of disease starts which may affect the newly emerged leaves. This disease spreads when the temperature is 20° to 24°C but even a temperature range of 6°C to 32°C is bad. The disease under suitable climate may complete its cycle in 5-6 days. Its relative humidity plays a destructive role with the spread of this powdery mildew disease. Under relative humidity from 70 % to 80%, the disease may spread very fast. But high relative humidity and very dim light with very low sunshine may also cause its spread.

4) Dead arm (*Phomopsis Viticola*):

This disease is caused by a fungus and occurs most frequently in table grape area the fungus lives throughout winter in disease-affected cane arms, spurs and petioles left on the vines; the infection occurs during the winter when the shoots are young. The disease spreads from the old disease area to young tissues by late spring rains. The angular spots often coalesce to form large brown areas with numerous dark spots. The diseases may cause canker in the older shoots and canes. The spread of the disease area on the cluster stem causes bunch rot with the fungus growing back into the wood of the arm and gradually kills the arm.

Control measures:

This disease is caused by (*Phomopsis Viticola*) the fungal Mycelium and spores persists on the canes and at relative humidity of 90 to 100% spread of the diseases starts on newly emerged leaves or it enters through air-injured portion. Later the vines get infected with the onset of rains through high wind. While taking up pruning the hands of labours who are engaged in pruning the vines, which are free from this disease, also get affected. After the entry of pathogen, symptoms starts being visible within a month. The disease requires 100 % relative humidity with 23° to 26°C temperature.

5) Diplodia Cane Blight:

This disease causes blighted area of green canes that are grey to brown with dark brown streaks projecting at the advanced margin of the blight canker. Grey areas are often speckled with numerous black dots.

Wounds, caused by girdling and pruning cuts on grapevine trunks, are sometimes infected by *Diplodia Natalensis*. Cankers develop under the bark, then the bark dries, cracks and peels away. A temperature of 30-35'C is most congenial. April pruning onwards, new sprouts emerge if rains occurs or the relative humidity reaches 80 % then development may take place.

6 Alternaria :

(*Alternaria alternata*) is a fungal disease and at the initial stage on leaves small yellowish spots are observed. Later they enlarge, and the leaf lamina may show leaf spots. If the disease is severe then leaf drop is noticed; during rainy seasons this disease is severe.

7) Leaf Spots: (*Cercospora Viticola*)

This is also a fungal disease, which you can observe on

the young shoots which is light in colour and spots are small in size. The spots on older leaves at margin, when there is severity, may spread to other leaves of the vine, then slowly the colour of spots become black. In an atmosphere where the relative humidity is 85% and above with a temperature of 25 to 26°C' may help in further spread immediately.

8 Bacterial blight (*Xanthomonas Compestris* pv. *vitis vinifera*)

This a bacterial disease; its first attack will be on young emerging leaves and young shoots. Small eruptions on young leaves at the lower surface on entire lamina will be observed and the infection is observed on veins then slowly the size of spots get enlarged to 0.5 mm to 2.5 mm where there are minute black spots or pointed spots or streaks. Slowly the spot on canes and on leaves petiole are observed. After pruning within 2-3 weeks, it enters the bottom of canes and enters. When the infected canes or branches are opened, inside we can see black spots in colour or discolouration.

Control measures:

This is caused by *Xanthomonas compestris* pv. *Vitis vinifera*. It enters from a injured portion and spreads to the entire plant system, which may remain for 200 days in the plant. The innoculum may move along with the metabolites or plasma in the entire plant system. So also insects, thunder storm, hail storm and a little temperature of 20 to 24° C may help in spread of the disease very fast.

Insect pest of grape

1. **Thrips - (*Rhipipherothrips cruentatus*)**

Thrips are the most trouble some insect pest of grape. They cause white patches on leaves of grape, curling of leaves and yellowing of blossom. There will be poor set with infested vine. They are also responsible for scab formentation of berries. This can be controlled by spraying 1 mda chloropid 0.3 ml/

litre Dimethoate 1.70 ml/litre oxy demeton 1 ml/litre.

2. **Flea beetle : (*Scelodonta strigicollis*)**

This also a major pest in grape. The grubs feed on the upper surface of the leaves and tender shoots and also attack roots. This can be controlled by spraying Imda chloropid 0.30 ml/lit, oxy demeton methyl 1 ml/liter, phophomidon o.5 ml/ lit.

3. **Vine Girdler (*Stethenias grisator*)**

These beetles are found during night. They make a girdle on the arms or on the main trunk in the initial stage and completely cut the vine. This can be controlled by swabing the bark by carbaryl 20 g/litre of water.

4. **Mealy bug (*Ferrisiana virgata*)**

Both nymph and aduls suck cell sap from the plant parts and berries. Infested portion are generally coated with a sticky honey dew on which sooty mould develop. If shoots are affected, it results in malformation of leaves and growing shoot tips, mealy bugs are effectively controlled by release of lady bird *Cryptolaemus montrouzieri, pullus alegans, Scymnus cocivora* on a large scale. A minimum of 600 beetles has to be released for an acre. Some time sticky substance like 'Tack Trap' or 'Bird tangle foot' may be applied either side of the shoot at the junction of the bunds Mealy bug can be controlled by spraying Applaud 1.25 ml + fish oil soap 5 gm/litre drencling with 1mda chloropid 2-3 ml/lit./plant. Spraying *Verticillium lacanii* 5g/ litre also help in controlling of mealy bug, or *Verticillium lacanii* should be mixed with vermi wash and applied through drip to over come mealy bug problem if the infestationis very severe then remove the bark of the vine and brush with tooth brush to clean the mealy bug, some time paste the tape one feet above the ground & on tape greese can be applied, but dont apply greese on main trunk otherwise the vine may die.

5. Mites

They suck the sap of the leaves, in severe case the leaves may dry. To controll this spray Dicofol 2ml/litre or Ethion 2 ml/lit or Wettable suphur 2 gm/litre of water.

6. Nematodes (*Meloidogyne incognita*)

The affected vine show slow decline in vigour with inadequarte sprouting after pruning. Apply Neem cake 500 gm/vine or Furadon 5 gm/vine to control nematode.

Chapter 12

Physiological Disorders in Grape

When grape is almost ready for harvest the physiological disorders starts exhibiting, viz., pink berry, shot berry, mummy, water berry etc.

We have to reduce the above problem and increase the quality.

Before the physiological symptoms start emerging, precautionary measures should be taken. While taking quality grape production, the symptoms appear slowly and by the time harvest completes its spreads on a large-scale, it results in reduction in yield but on a large-scale quality deteriorates and such quality affects bunches which are not fit for export and for local market ultimately the farmer won't get the price as per his expectation.

This kind of physiological disorders have no relationship with pests and diseases. The following are the commonly observed physiological disorders in grape production:

1) Small round berries - shot berries
2) Thickly accumulated berries - water berries
3) Drying of berries (mummification) - stalk necrosis
4) Reddish/pinkish berries - pink berries
5) Hard/stiff berry pedicel - stiffing stalk
6) Bunch scorching - scorching.

Among the above listed physiological problems one or more than one physiological disorders are observed in small or high proportion in a bunch.

The cause for physiological disorders:

While berry development and when its development stops the ripening starts. If there is a change in the climatic fluctuation then such physiological disorders are observed and develops. Especially when fluctuations in the temperature and relative humidity are observed.

Defective soil and water:

If there is a problem in soil and water analysis reports like Ec, pH etc., then the berry development will be affected. Due to which physiological disorders comes to the picture.

3) Improper Use of Fertilizer:

Unless you understand the hunger of crops and which element, available nutrients and which fertilizer is suitable, you wont get proper yield. The improper foliar application of nutrients results in physiological disorders.

4) Improper Use of Growth Regulators:

Early application of growth regulators, without its needs and wrong selection of growth regulators, physiological disorders are increased.

5) Improper Application of Insecticide and Fungicides:

While controlling pests and diseases, wrong selection of fungicide, combinations of fungicides and wrong application method results in increase of physiological disorders.

6 Watering/Irrigation:

Irregular/improper application of irrigation/watering during bunch development may increase the physiological problem.

7) Time and application:

While thinning, girdling, tipping, if there is any delay,

physiological disorders are observed. Physiological disorders may occur due to many reasons and for every physiological disorder, control measures should be taken in time. If not taken, then the problem aggravates or the other physiological disorders symptoms are observed.

Physiological Disorder and its Control Measures: Climatic Factors:

1) Temperature:

During bunch development if climate is not suitable such as low temperature, then night smoking is advised in closed confinement by erecting artificial curtains or wind breaks.

2) Relative humidity:

At berry development a RH of 60-70% RH or more and at ripening period aRH of 50'-60% or less is desirable. But at berry development (more than) 80% relative humidity and RH < (less than) 45 % will effect berry development. If at ripening period RH increases then berry cracking is observed. To reduce relative humidity, stir the soil, reduce irrigation quantity and how much quantity of water you require for foliar spray depends on incidence of control of pest and diseases.

3) Quality of Soil and Water:

In more number of places, the upper layer contains more of salt for example calcium, sodium, potassium and magnesium but during rainy season the salt gets leached away from the root zone. During berry development if there is shortage of water the salt gets accumulated in between the root zone, which spoils the nutrient uptake. If soil is good and water is bad, containing chloride, then also it will have lot of problems. In some soils the top layer becomes hard and such soils are problematic soils for grape cultivation because of improper aeration. In due course of time physiological disorders appear. In soils where more than 10% lime nodules are noticed the production of quality grapes become very difficult. Therefore a period between April pruning to October pruning, apply green manure to reduce bad effect of lime nodules. In such grape garden after October pruning, while giving open well irrigation, first remove the existing open well water completely. Then recouped new fresh water which may be utilized for irrigation.

Such soils and open well water or bore well water after October pruning should be tested in the laboratory and as per recommendation, it should be used.

Soil nematodes and other harmful microbes should be kept under control.

4) Balanced Fertilizer Application:

To avoid physiological disorders, apply fertilizers with care. As per soil testing report, ascertain the available nutrient in soil whether it is optimum or not for cultivation. Then select the fertilizer. In problematic soils and soil affected with lime nodules don't apply super phosphate, murate of potash and complex fertilizers viz., 19:19:19, 15:15:15, 17:17:17 etc. In lime nodule; affected plot if you apply super phosphate, then it forms calcium phosphate that will get fixed in the soil specially phosphorus which is not available to develop bunches. With the application of murate of potash chloride deposits, it affects the bunch quality. If potash nutrient application is of more than required quantity then physiological disorders aggravate, and application of complex fertilizers may result in set-backs.

Therefore to get quality fruits and to avoid physiological disorders complex fertilizer application should be avoided.

Timely application of fertilizers with required quantity is important to observe crop condition. If growth is slow then petiole analysis becomes a must. Among the major nutrient (NPK), nitrogen in the beginning stage, phosphorus in the middle stage and later, potash is required and their balanced application from time to time is very important.

Water berries are noticed in a bunch under the situation when nitrogen is applied in large quantity or nitrogen is applied more than its requirement or applied at later stages when berries are of pea size. During flowering, the petiole should be examined thoroughly because if there is a deficiency of calcium stalk necrosis and stalk, stiffening may occur.

In most of the soils of Karnataka calcium is available in abundant quantity but it won't reach the bunches; as a result there will be more demand for potash, which results in reduction of calcium availability and uptake.

Deficiency of calcium before October pruning if found in vine then phloem becomes more. In the beginning, if availability of calcium is less and potash is more then Phloem along with Xylem function will be hampered which will not be visible to the naked eye. During nutrition, excess application of potash hampers cane growth. For grape quality, such as sugar percentage and colour development, potash is required. At the time of berry development, fertilizer without potash, are not desirable. Application of murate of potash in place of sulphate of potash increases the chloride level which will be a set-back to grape production and quality. If potash availability is more, then the demand for magnesium increases. When potash demand is fulfiled then deficiency symptoms of magnesium starts exhibiting, when demand of magnesium increases then calcium availability becomes problematic; then to fulfil the demand of soil for magnesium and calcium, apply calmag and take up foliar spray also. For soil application, apply calmag at October pruning and at fruit set take up foliar spray.

If requirement of leaf and calcium, magnesium is brought under control as calcium content in bunches and berry pedicel may not improve so easily since translocation of magnesium in leaf is easy.

When calcium problem is solved then physiological

disorders can be rectified. Deficiency of zinc, boron increases the physiological disorder. During this period the climate should be mild with sunshine period of 12 hours and there should not be much difference between minimum and maximum temperatures. Night temperature, if it is 15°C, then day temperature should be around 30°C. If temperature is more, then take spraying of water. If night temperature is low then by smoking try to increase the night temperature. If sunshine hours are less then install tubelight for that period.

Low temperature and fog will have bad effect on the berry development, only possible solution is to have wind-break plan with smoking of the garden. At berry ripening period, low relative humidity, medium temperature and full sunshine is helpful, which prevails after 15th January. But if ripening starts earlier than in the second fortnight of January it can cause problems. Under such situation spraying of some hormone will be of some help like CCC 250 ppm to 500 ppm and within completion of a week, Kinetin, Uracil or 6 BA 5 to 10 ppm foliar spray helps to overcome the shortage of sunlight.

Bunch Quality and Nutrient Management:

One has to understand yield and fertigation, its co-relation to get good quality. If you apply less nutrients, yield is affected, the effect of nutrient on yield can be seen immediately but on quality it shows late.

Control of nitrogen application:

Nitrogen is important to increase yield as well as quality. Excess application of nitrogen has effect on yield as well as on quality. Less application of nitrogen reduces yield but improves quality. Excess application of nitrogen reduces the potash uptake and ripening will be delayed. In a bunch, berries at the tip show improper sugar development with berries being bigger or smaller in size. The colour of berries at ripening shows light greenish colour rather than golden yellow. In a bunch one side of the berries are greenish and the other side are yellowish in colour. Late application of nitrogen causes pre-harvest and post-harvest berry drop problem.

After October pruning, application of optimum doses of nitrogen is very important at flowering, berry development and ripening stages.

At bunch development, if nitrogen availability is less then yield gets reduced. If nitrogen availability is more then the quality deteriorates. If nitrogen applied through leaves results will be quicker than soil application but when it is applied through soil it should be in split doses. For export quality grape, after October pruning, nitrogen has to be applied in ten stages that is before flowering for two times and at berry development four times. When it is in sink stage, three times and at the beginning of ripening one time; if necessary totally ten times. At the first stages irrigate through drip in two days interval. At second stage daily, third stage alternate day and fourth stage every fourth day. On the third and fourth stages nitrogen through foliar can be given.

Nitrogen levels (%)

Bunch stage	Low yield 20-25 ton/ha	Medium yield 25-30 ton/ha	High yield 30-35 ton/ha
Full bloom	1.20 to 1.75	1.70 to 2.50	2.10 to 2.50
Berry development (fast period)	1.50 to 1.75	2.10 to 2.50	1.40 to 2.98
Berry development (slow period)	1.30 to 1.50	2.0 to 2.25	2.20 to 2.60
Beginning of ripening, full ripening	1.20 to 1.40 1.00 to 1.10	1.80 to 2.0 1.40 to 1.60	1.80 to 2.20 1.40 to 1.80

Ammonium sulphate, urea can be used for folair spray in ammonical and nitrogen forms.

Use more organic manure, zinc chelated, ferrous chelated as a foliar spray to overcome the problems of berries and pink berries. Give zinc for slow development of berry and at ripening stage boron demand is more. If soil temperature comes down then zinc and boron availability also get reduced. However during this period if you apply more of nitrogen and phosphorus, then availability of zinc boron also reduces.

Proper Use of Growth Hormones:

Among the growth regulators, improper use of Gibberlic acid is also responsible for the physiological disorders. More use of GA at flowering stage results in thickening and hardening of berries and berry pedicel. So when GA is used in more concentration the physiological disorders may be noticed. After GA application demand for boron increases. Deficiency of boron is observed at terminal leaves and on berries. If you apply boron by keeping more leaves in front of the bunch and less berries in a bunch then more damage is noticed. When the berries start ripening use foliar spray of boron. If you apply more GA at this stage then take up spraying of lihocin or NAA. CCC will reduce the effect of GA and NAA to stop dissolving of berries, for which first spray of 200-250 ppm of CCC, later 25 to 40 ppm of NAA, is helpful.

Before the physiological disorder problem arises, careful or precautionary measures are necessary from fruit set to pea size berry development.

Quantity Attainment:

Increasing grape productivity is one part while to improve the grape quality is another part, but to have both qualities at one go is very difficult. If the yield is low then quality definitely improves but is doubtful, whereas per hectare, what should be the yield one must be able to understand very easily. First, one has to understand what is quality. The grape which is going to be exported to a particular country and its quality parameters are required to be understood by the farmers.

The common understanding is to go for high yield with low quality but low yield with good quality is not proper. When you think of export then keep a target of 25-30 tonnes per hectare.

Grape quality parameters:

1) Grape berry - long and oval.
2) Berry colour - greenish
3) Berry TSS - 20 to 22 %
4) Berry juice-70-90 %
5) Berry acidity-0.6 %
6) Berry sugar : acidity-36:1 to 40 :1
7) Berry peri carp - thin and crispy
8) Berry shape - triangular
9) Juice taste - pleasant taste
10) No. of berries in a bunch - 125 to 150
12) Berry pedicel- thick, long, greenish and strong
13) Berry thickness - 18 to 20 mm
14) Bunch weight - 400 to 600 gm
15) Bunch appearance - fresh and pleasing. The grape quality parameters are more but each item is of importance.

The post harvest quality parameters are:

1) After harvest, its shelf life is important.
2) Post-harvest berry drop should be less.
3) There should not be any spot or insecticide/fungicide
4) Chemical residues should not cross its limit.
5) Total grape bunches should suffice the variety in demand.
6) It should fit all the export parameters.

Suitable Climate for Grape Production:

To get good grape per hectare tonnage, which grape variety we have to grow one has to understand and also in which season/month it should come for harvest to meet the export demand should be known. Season means climate i.e., temperature, relative humidity and sunlight-these three factors are very important. Establishment of flower primordial, berry development and its ripening are three important development stages and each stage is totally different from each other and like-wise climatic requirements also vary. From flowering to fruit set it requires 15 days. During that period the temperature requirement should be minimum of 15 to 16° C and maximum of 30 to 32° C with relative humidity of 60 % with 11 hours of sunlight. Then later comes the berry development in which two stages are involved. First stage is of early development which is of three weeks then second stage of sink or rest period which is of few hours or of 2 to 3 days. Then again berry development starts which lasts for three weeks. So totally it is a period of 5-6 weeks.

Chapter 13

Processing

Raisin:

The grapes meant for raisin making should preferably be seedless, white, with thin skin and TSS above 24 Brix. Select fully ripe bunches and remove damaged and diseased berries. Selected bunches are dipped in a boiling NaOH (Caustic Soda) solution of 0.3 per cent for 3 Sec. followed by cold water washing. Treated bunches are spread on perforated trays, kept in an air tight sulphur box and fumigated by burning sulphur at the rate of 3g/kg of fresh grape for 3 hours. Sulphyited bunches may either be dried in a hot air drier at 60 - 65°C temeperature or they may be allowed to dry under shade at room temperature till the raisins get about 15 per cent moisture content. Soon after drying raisins should be separated from dried rachies quickly and thoroughly washed in lukewarm water, air dried and kept for moisture equalisation for a period of one month in an air tight container. Afterwards, raisins are packed in 400 gauge polythene bags and stored at cool temperature (3-5°C). IIHR variety 'Arkavati' has been found to be better for raisin making.

Seeded white grapes with high total soluble solids (TSS) may be used for making 'Munnaca' while coloured grapes like Beauty Seedless can be used for making black raisins to be used in confectionery. (Fig)

SODA OIL DIPPED RAISIN

Seedless grapes are dipped ina sodium solution having a thin film layer of oilve on the surface, the dipped grapes are dried in trays in direct sunlight. The raisins are medium to dark brown in colour, fairly tender, slightly oily but not sticky. The grapes are dipped in warm solution containing 3 kg cooking soda and 100g sodium hydroxide in 100 ltr of water for 3 minutes on which1 ltr of olive oil is floated. After removing from the dipping solution the grapes are dried in sun.

In another method grapes are immersed in a water solution containing 4.5 percent potassium carbonated, 0.5% sodium carbonate and 1% completely emulsified olive oil for about five minutes. The grapes are spread in trays and turned in trays after two days.

The Austrailin method involves dipping of grape in alkaling emulsion of commercial dipping oil which is mixture of about 70% ethyl esters with free oleic acid emulsifiers.

1. Standard cold dip emulsion :

Potassium carbonates	2.4 kg
Dipping oil	1.5 ltr
Water	100 ltr

2. Standard cold dip

emulsion (Two third)	1.7 kg
Dipping oil	1.0 ltr
Water	100 ltr

Trimmed and washed bunches in perforated plastic crates are dipped in water containing the commercial dipping oil (a mixture of potassium carbonate and ethyl oleate) The required quality of dipping oil is poured in water in a cement tank to raise the pH of the solution to 10. The pH is tested with litmus paper, grape trays are allowed in the dipping solution for five minutes and taken out draining the solution completely, the grapes are spread on fine mesh (1 cm x 1 cm) nylon nets stretched in tiers, of nylon nets with a clearance of 9" to 10" between two successive one and built in sheds with tin roof. Drying completes in 10 days.

Chapter 14

Wine Making

Wine is fermented juice of fresh fruits. It is considered as a health drink composed of water, alcohol, pigments, esters, vitamins, carbohydrates, minerals, acids, tannins with medicinal and therapeutic values. Generally it is found that a quart of vine with 10 per cent alcohol gives about 850 calories of energy, that is, approximately equivalent to a pound of meat or 20 ounce of milk. Inspite of its quality, the wine market in India is still considered recent with hard liquor claiming a huge chunk of the market. In western countries wine has been a part of the diet and represented as a safe and healthy beverage. In India Govt. regulations make wine making and wine marketing an obstacle. Like Maharashtra state other state Govt. should also modify and simplify the modes and regulations of wine industry.

In Indian Rigveda there is a mention of vine as 'Somarasa' Ayurvedic medicines are prepared in the media of fermented fruit juices.

In recent days Indians have started appreciating wine. The upper class Indian is convinced that good food has to be accompanied by wine. Wine consumption has doubled in the last 2-3 years, the wine-pubs like beer-pubs have started appearing in Indian metropolitan cities. Indian wine lovers are realising that a good wine can very well match with deshi Indian food.

As climatic conditions in India are suitable for growing a number of different varieties of wine grapes, best Indian wines can be made from a blend of grape varieties. By addition of cardamom, cloves, and other spices medicated wines or vermouths can be prepared to popularize wine culture in India so that they can be better accepted. A wine cocktail can be prepared by mixing a bottle of wine with sugar and fruits like orange, apple and maccrated for two hours before serving. Such kind of experiments can bring wine culture in India. So that India starts moving away from hard liquor and discover the pleasure in savouring delicate wines with Indian deshi foods. Similarly wines can be prepared from various tropical fruits like pomegranate, pineapple, sapota etc.,

Scope for Indian Wines

India produces over 6.5 million tons of fruits every year and nearly 30-40 per cent fruits may loose their marketability due to undersized fruits, spotted fruits, cracked fruits, immature fruits and post-harvest losses accounts for around 2.5 million tons. Such losses can be validated by preparing wine out of such fruits. By considering 50 per cent juice from such fruits, it can be converted into wine as value added product for local markets. A good quality wine can be prepared from pomegranate, apple, pineapple etc.,

Export of Wines:

The European market is the main consumer of wine with its own quality standards. European union had prohibited import of wine from Third World countries. The European union in its regulation no. 1470/1990 of July 5th 1999 has amended regulation number 3201/90 giving detailed rules for the description and presentation of wine and grape. The European Union has accepted the Indian request and India has appeared in the list of countries that can export wines to European Union. The European Commission has notified "Central Food Technological Institute" (CFTRI) Mysore, as the Indian agency for pre-shipment inspection, as per EI regulation of February 1999. The wine to be exported to European union will have to be certified by CFTRI. However, the approved varieties of wine grape is enlisted for wine making. The Indian wine exporters can get their names enlisted in the list of wine exporters from Ministry of Commerce, Govt., of India.

Wineries of India:

The Growers winery located in Ragunathpura in Doddaballapur taluk in Bangalore district of Karnataka is one of the main wineries in Karnataka Shaw Wallace winery. In Hyderabad in Andhra Pradesh there has been an important winery producing 'Golconda' wine. The area under grape is maximum in Maharashtra state. In recent times the prices for table grapes and resins has come down and Govt. of Maharashtra has promoted the wine Industries. The M/s Indage India (M/s Champagne India) Narayanagaon, Baramati winery in Baramati, SULA winery in Nasik, Indogrape winery in Pandarapur are some of the main wineries in Maharashtra. The new wineries are coming up in Maharashtra.

Viti-culture for Wine Makers:

It is often said that great wines are made in vineyards. The industry of the world is built upon one species i.e. Vitis Vinifera. L. While selecting a wine variety the important trails to be considered are its tractability, distinctive flavour, special characters and economics of sales, etc. It is found that highly calcareous soils produce best quality wines. However, the new planting of wine grape varieties should be taken up on root stocks. Among various root stocks are Dogridge-A, Dogridge B, Ramsay (Salt Creek), Saint George, etc. Dogridge-B is found to be more suitable. The rootstock improves the vigour, fruiting canes, drought tolerance and will develop ability to leach out harmful ions. To get better quality of wine grape nutrients are to be replenished organically rather than inorganically alone. Yield levels should not exceed 6-7 tons/acre.

Wine grape varities:

Red wine varieties	White wine varieties.
1. Zinfandel	1. Chardonnay
2. Cabernet-sauvignon	2. Chennin blanc
3. Grenache	3. Sauvignon-blanc
4. Pinot Noir	4. Riesling-white
5. Ruby red	5. Pinot-blanc
6. Marlot	6. Muscat-blanc
7. Ruby cabernet	7. Colombard
8. Carignon	8. Ugni-blanc

Characteristics of Grape required for Making Different Types of Wines:

Type of wine	Degree Bric	Titrable acidity g, tartaric/lit	pH
Sparkling wine	18-20.0	7.0-9.0	2.8-3.2
White table wine	19.5-23.0	7.0-8.0	3.0-3.3
Red label wine	20.5-23.5	6.5-7.5	3.2-3.4
Sweet table wine	22.0-25.0	6.5-8.0	3.2-3.4
Dessert wine	23.0-26.0	5.0-7.5	3.3-3.7

Different Types of Wine:

Wine generally contain alcohol in the range of 8-16%. Depending upon its sugar content, alcohol content are of various types of wines as dry wine, fortified, wine, spiraling wine etc.,

Dry wine: A wine in which all the sugar of juices are practically fermented.

Sweet Wine: A wine in which some of the sugar is left unfermented or additional sugar is added after fermentation.

Fortified wine: A wine to which brandy or some other alcoholic spirit is added after the fermentation. E.g. Sherry, Port Wine contains 17-23 % alcohol.

Sparkling wine: A wine in which considerable amount of CO_2 is present arising fermentation directly in the bottle. It is also called as carbonated wine E.g. champagne contain 11-12 %.

Red wine: A wine made from the red grapes wherein the pomace (skins, seeds & pieces of stems) is left during fermentation, strong flavour is because of tannins from grape skin e.g. Burgundy.

White wine: A wine that is prepared from white grapes or from the juice of red grapes from which the pomace is removed.

Home wine-making:

Wine making at home is more of an art rather than science. Any good Indian cook can become easily an oncologist. Many times home made wines are sold in hotels at costly price than wines made from wineries. The whole procedure of wine making is given step-by-step for the easy adoption of methodology.

Preparation of Starter Culture:

A wine yeast culture of *Saccharomyces ellipsoideus* maintained on Yeast Extract peptone Dextrose Agar (YEPD). A loopful inoculum of wine yeast culture is transferred into a test tube containing 5ml of YEPD broth and incubated overnight at 25°C. (The YEPD broth can be prepared by adding 10g of yeast extract 20g of peptone and 20g of dextrose to one litre of water and adjusting the pH to 5.4 before autoclaving.) The 5ml yeast culture is further added to 100 ml sterilized grape juice (5 % inoculum) in 250 ml flask and kept for incubation at 25° C for 22 hours on a shaking incubator at 120 rpm. This can be used to inoculate the fermentor after activating the yeast cells at 40° C for 1.5 hours.

Preparation of juice/must.

The fruits are either crushed by hand or by using pulpier. The extracted juice or pulp is called "must". If the fruit pulp contains more pectin then pectin's enzyme is added at 0.5% level and kept for incubation at 40°C for 3-4 hours for clarification of the juice.

Amelloration:

The must/juice should be tested for its sugar content and total acidity. The pH should be adjusted between 3.2-3.3; if the pH of the juice is still lower the acidity can be reduced with calcium carbonate or sodium bicarbonate (baking soda). If the pH value is on the higher side, tartaric acid or citric acid can be added. If juice/must is diluted the total soluble solids (TSS) has to be raised to 22-24 brix by adding sugar.

Addition of SO_4

Addition of potassium metabisulphite (KMS) is done at the rate of 200 PPM (100 PPM SO_2). However, after addition of KMS, allow a gap of about 3-4 hours before inoculating the must with wine yeast.

Fermentation:

The must is filled in the laboratory fermentor to its 3/4th capacity and inoculated with desired activated yeast culture @ 5 %. The lab fermentor or flasks or glass bottles must be equipped with air locking facility. In industries or wineries it is often accomplished for filling a fermentory with a special one-way value. The fermentation is allowed to carry out at 21 to 24° C. Temperature regulation is very important as finest quality wines are produced at lower temperatures. The air lock during fermentation is provided to prevent the acetification i.e., conversion of alcohol into vinegar.

Siphoning/Racking:

After allowing fermentation for 7 to 8 days–(2 to 3) days in case of red grape to reduce tannin content. The clean liquid is siphoned or racked from the sediment called "less" which contains the skin, seeds, yeast cells, organic precipitate etc. This can also be achieved by filtering through muslin cloth. The fermentation is allowed to continue for another two weeks. It can be racked once again to remove the sediments and filled in the bottles. The bottles can be stored in the refrigerator for maturation.

Maturation:

The newly–made wine is harsh in taste and has yeasty flavour. The process of maturation makes the wine tasty and fruity in flavour besides clarification. After storing in refrigerator for one week, racking is repeated and stored again in the refrigerator. Racking is repeated for 2 to 3 times at an interval of 15-20 days. Racking can be continued further at monthly intervals. During interacting period no headspace should be kept in the bottle and should be closed tightly. The period of maturation may extend to over a year in case of pigmented wines. The matured wines can be pasteurized and stored for long time at 15 to 16°C for again. The aging is a complex process in which precipitation of the suspended solids take place besides the formation of steps that impart the fruit flavour to the wine. Usage of oak wood chips during maturation is used for grape wine making. The wood chips are also used again for other fruit wines.

Sl. No	Items	Pomegranate	Grape
1	Cost of 1 kg fruits (Rs)	10.00	20.00
2	Yield of juice in ml/kg fruit	500.00	700.00
3	Cost of added chemical (Rs)	2.00	1.00
4	Processing cost (1/3 of raw material cost in Rs)	4.00	7.00
5	Wine yield from 1 kg fruit in ml	400.00	600.00
6	Cost of one litre of wine (Rs)		

Wine and Health:

1. An occasional wine drinking for a glass of wine a day is said to stave off neuro-degenerative diseases such as Alzheimer's and Parkinsons.
2. Alcohol concentration in wine may not be anti-microbial but phenolic compounds present in wine which are anti-microbial and helps in preventing many diseases like dysentery, diarrhoea and have protective effects against cardiovascular diseases.
3. There is positive correlation found between moderate wine consumption and improved health is possible due to decrease in the prevalence of age-related muscular degeneration.
4. The consumption of moderate amount of wine can reduce the risk of certain type of cancer diseases and increased consumption may provide some cancer diseases.
5. Moderate wine consumers may live on an average 2.5 years longer than teetotallers and considerably longer than heavy drinkers.

Tips to Wine Drinkers:

1. Most homemade wines are good to have when they are atleast a year old. They normally stay well for 3-4 years.
2. It is not necessary to finish your bottle of wine the day you open it. It keeps well for 2-3 weeks with airtight stoppers.
3. Never keep your wine bottle at room temperature. The ideal temperature is between 12 to 15 degree centigrade. The bottle can simply be kept in refrigerator.
4. Occasional drinking or a glass of wine a day is found to be good for health.

(Courtesy Dr. A.B. Patil, AC- Bijapur).

Chapter 15

Breeding in Grape

Grapes belong to the genus *Vitis* of the family Vitaceae. The genus *Vitis* is divided into 2 sub-genera, namely, *Euvitis* and *Muscadinia.* There are nearly 57 species under *Euvitis* and 3 species, namely, *rotundifolia, munsoniana* and *popenodi* under *Muscadinia.* Besides differing in other characteristics, the *Euvitis* has a somatic chromosome complement of 38, while the *Muscadinia* has 40. Among all the species, *Vitis vinifera,* the Old World Grape, of the subgenus *Euvitis* is the most important as more than 90% of the grape varieties grown in the world today are derived directly or indirectly from this species. Other important species of *Euvitis* are *V. labrusca, V. cineria, V. riparia* and *V. rupestris. V. rotundifolia* is the most important species of the sub-genus *Muscadinia.* This is practically immune to diseases and pests including phylloxera and nematodes.

There are 3 main commercial uses of grapes, namely, table, raisin and wine. Grapes are also used for juice purpose which is unfermented. For breeding, definite objective should be kept in mind. The objectives vary from place to plage, e.g., for North India, earliness is very important, i.e. the varieties should ripen before the onset of monsoon rains in June. For south India, disease resistance is very important. This is in addition to high yield and good quality. The general objective of grape breeding is to develop high quality, high yielding and disease resistant varieties for specific purposes like table, raisin, wine and juice. For table varieties, seedlessness, large berry size, loose cluster and good colour are important characters. Raisin grapes should be seedless with good texture. Wine grapes should be high yielding and disease and insect resistant. In foreign countries like U.S.A., France and Germany, where there are phylloxera and nematode problems, breeding for rootstocks is also important. The rootstocks should be vigorous and resistant to nematodes and phylloxera. In our country, breeding rootstocks for resistant to salinity and drought is important.

Grape as Breeding Material and Breeding System

The *vinifera* grape has originated in the region between Black and Caspian seas in Middle Asia. To being with, the native vine was dioecious with the male and female vines occurring in about equal numbers. Rarely a male vine, at least in some species, may produce a few hermaphroditic flowers and some fruits, so that vines may in this sense be considered subdioecious. Female vines, on the other hand, have not been known to revert to the other sexual types. Breeding results based on many varieties and species, that the simple genetic explanation for the 3 sexual types (0, 0 & 0) of grapevine can be formulated on a multiple hypothesis at a single locus, a follows:

Male vine	: Su F Sum
Devied males	: Su F Su F, Su F Su +
Female	: Su m, Sun
Homozygous from a phordite	: Su + Su+
Heterozygous from a phrodite	: Su+ Su m

The dominance relationship of the 3 alleles is thus:

SuF> Su+ > Sum.

The native vine was originally cross-pollinating, but sėlection for hermophrodite or female types)the only ones to produce fruits) must have occurred very early. As larger vineyards and single varieties were selected and established, in more isolated areas, even the female varieties were really discarded because of partial or complete failure to be cross-pollinated.

The grapes are highly heterozygous. The heterozygosity at first was maintained sexually at a higher level by enforced cross-pollination to produce new varieties. Added to this are the long periods of asexual propagation and an accumulating mutational load to further increase heterozygosity. In the world collection of varieties, there are no varieties of any importance that can trace their origin to selfing of a parental variety. Inbreeding results in rapid loss of vine vigour and fertility, even a in the first generation.

The most useful breeding method is crossing of unrelated parents with good combining ability followed by raising a large number of hybrid seedlings in each combination and rigorous selection in F1. Test crossing with a common parent is also useful in exploring the genetic potential of a large number of varieties. The aim is to produce the maximum state of useful heterozygosity since many selection can be quickly and easily reproduced by asexual means.

BREEDING METHODS

1. *Introduction ad Selection*

In breeding, introduction of germplasm from various sources is the first step. Selection of introductions best suited to local condition is one of the methods of breeding. In India, the first extensive collection of *vinifera* varieties was assembled at Lyallpur in the Pubjap before partition of the country. They found 7 varieties out of 116 as promising. These varieties were, however, lost to Pakistan after partition. Collection were then made at Ganeshkhind Fruit Research Station, Pune; Horticultural Research Institute, Sahranpur; Indian Agricultural Research Institute, new Delhi and Indian Institute of Horticultural Research, Hessaraghatta, Bangalore. Perlette is the most outstanding selection made for North India. It ripens before the onset of Monsoon. Other promising selection are Beauty Seedless, Himrod and Delight.

At I.I.H.R., Bangalore, nearly 1000 grape varieties and 20 *vitis* species were collected. They were evaluated thoroughly for various purposes like table, raisin, wine and juice. Ten varieties were found to be promising for fresh table purpose, 8 varieties for dry white table wine, 12 varieties for dry red table wine, 2 varieties for red dessert wine and 2 varieties for raisin making. The varieties are:

Fresh table purpose: Angur Kalan, Athens, Black Champa, Coarna Rosie, Convent Large Black, Medeleine Celine, Red Prince, Katta Kurgan, Queen of the Vineyrads and Taifi Rozovi.

Dry white table wine: Bayan Shirei, Chenin blanc, Excelsior, Fateasca Alba, Ova Pagola, S.V. 5276, Sauvignon and White Riesling.

Dry red table wine: Black Champa, Black Cornichon, Black Muscat, Convent, Large Black, Gamsa, Fateasca Neagra, Muscat, Red Prince, Rubired, Saperavi, Tievoasa and Zinfandel.

Red dessert wine: Black Champa and Convent Large Black.

Raisin purpose: Thompson Seeless and Black Corinth.

II. Intervarietal Hybridization

A large number of hybrids were raised and evaluated at IIHR, Balgalore and IARI, New Delhi. At I.I.H.R., Balgalore, 4 very promising hybrids were named and released for cultivation. They are: 1. Arkavati, 2. Arka Kanchan, 3. Arka Shyam and 4. Arka Hans.

Arkavati: It is a hybrid between Black Champa and Thompson Seedless. It is seedless with good quality (T.S.S. 22-25%, acidity 0.6-0.7%). it is excellent for making raisins and good for making champagne, dry white table wine and also for fresh table purpose. It has yielded up to 30 tonnes per acre as against 12 tonnes per acre in Thompson Seedless.

Arka Kanchan It is from a cross of Anab-e-Shahi and Queen of the Vineyards. Seeded with good muscat flavour. T.S.S. 19-

22% and acidity 0.5-0.6%. It is good for making dry and sweet table and dessert (Muscatel) wines.

Arka Shyam: This hybrid is from a cross of Bangalore Blue and Black Champa. Seeded with good quality (T.S.S. 22-25%, acidity 0.5-0.6%). Resistant to anthracnose. Two crops can be taken in a year in southern and western India. It is good for making juice and for making dry and sweet table wines.

Arka Hans: It is a hybrid between Balgalore Blue and Anab-e-Shahi. Seeded with good quality (T.S.S. 18-21%, acidity 0.4-0.5%). Resistant to anthracnose Double cropping possible in peninsular India. It is good for making wines.

All the above 4 varieties produce good cross on bower as well as head system of training.

At IARI, New Delhi, 3 early ripening hybrids have been developed, which are under testing.

Dr. G.S. Cheema from Ganeshkhind F.R.S., Poona, planted naturally cross-pollinated seeds of Pandhari Sahebi (0 sterile) and obtained 2 new varieties, Selection-7 and S-94. S-7 is now called Cheema Sahebi. These varieties have had some success in grape industry, especially around Poona. Their major defect is poor keeping quality.

In U.S.A.: Some of the important varieties developed by Prof. H.P. Olmo and released by Davis, California are as follows.

1. Perlettee: Queen of the Vineyards x Sultaniana Marble
2. Delight : Queen of the Vineyards x Sultanina Marble
3. Deauty Seedless : Queen of the Vineyards x Black Kishmish
4. Ruby Cabernet : Carignane x Cabernet Sauvignon
5. Emerald Riesling ; Muscadelle x White Riesling
6. Rubired : Alicante Ganzin x Tinto Cao
7. Royalty ; Alicante Ganzin x Trousseau

8. Scarlet : Golden Muscat x Teinturier

9. Niabell : Niagara x Campbell Early

(IV) (IV)

Varieties released by U.S..D.A, Fresno

1. Cardinal : Flame Tokay x Alponse Lavellee

2. Calmeria : resulted from seeds of open-pollinated Ohanez (Almeria)

3. Black Rose : (Damas Rose x Black Momukka) x Alphonse Lavallee.

In U.S.S.R.: late Prof. A.M. Negrual developed 16 varieties, which are given below:

1. Tarnau (Seedless) : Nimrang x Kishmish Chiorni
2. Volgo-Don : Katta Kurgan x Zabalkaski
3. Djura Izum : Nimrang x Taifi Rozovi
4. Pabeda : Zbalkanski x Muscat Hamburg
5. Rani VIR a : Chauch x Kishmish Chiorni
6. Muscat VIRa : Muskat Beli x Muskat Hamburg
7. Oktyabraski : Nimrang x Kabarnai
8. Maskat Uzbekistanski : Charas x Muskat Hamburg
9. Charas Muskatski : Charas x Muskat Hamburg
10. Pozdni VIR a : Nimrang x dobrelyabi
11. Guzel Kara : Katta Kurgan x Dobrelyabi
12. VIR Adin : Takveri x Tibushe
13. Prima : (Muskat Alexandriski x Pufliakovski x *V. rupestris*)
14. Salava : Tagobi x Amuski
15. Uzbekistan : (Tagobi x Amurski) x Tagobi

16. Perri May : Tinturye x Aleatiko

III. *Interspecific Hybridization*

All the species within the subgenus *Euvitis* cross readily. In North America, the spontaneosu and intentional hybridization of *V. vinifera* with *V. labrusca* resulted in evolution of *American Hybrids* such as Concord, Catawba and Isabella. These hybrids are hardy and more resistant to diseases than *vinifera* varieties. These varieties are grown commercially in Easter U.S., Japan and also in China.

When the rootlouse, phylloxera, decimated the vineyards in France and other countries of Europe, American species, namely *V. rupestris, V. lincecumii* and *V. riparia* were introduced to France. The private French grape breeders attempted crosses involving these species and *V. vinifera* to create a "direct producer", a vine having phylloxera resistance and also good wine quality. This quest was such as Seibel 1000, Seyve-Villard 5276 emerged. These hybrids are more resistant to diseases and are capable of higher production than *vinifera*. These hybrids are easily identified by the breeders name. These hybrids occupy one fifth of a total vineyard acreage of France and produce average quality wine. These are outlawed in other parts of the world as their wine quality is poor.

An Oriental *Vitis* species, *V. amurensis* of Siberia has been used by Russians to impart cold resistance to the *vinifera* grape.

Native species of *Euvitis* are confined almost entirely to the North Temperate zone. However, one species called *Vitis caribea* has been found growing in abundance in the tropical Caribbean area. In Venezuella, this vine has hybridized spontaneously with the poorly adapted *vinifera* to produce a new race of very vigorous and disease resistance vines locally called "Criollas". These may be very useful for improving tropical viticulture.

So in *Euvitis,* there is no serious bars to gene exchange. In wider or intergeneric cross between *rotundifolia* of the subgenus *Muscadinia* and *vinifera,* thus exists a unilateral type of incompatibility. Varieties of *Vitis vinifera* can be successfully and easily crossed with the pollen from various clones of *rotundifolia,* but all reciprocal combinations fail. This failure is not due to lack of pollen tube growth but must reside in the cytoplasm of the embryo sac or maternal tissue bordering the embryo sac. The F_1 hybrid of *vinifera-rotundifolia* crosses are uniform and vigorous, but they are with few exceptions completely pollen and ovule sterile. Some hybrids have shown to carry high resistance of immunity to phylloxera and could be used rootstocks. The particular *vinifera* varieties used as female parent is very important it determines to a large extent the number of viable seeds obtained. Success have then been achieved in obtaining family fertile forms. Then diploid *vinifera x rotundifolia* hybrids are expected to be of great value in the transfer of diseases and insect resitance into the *vinifera* group as *V. rotundifolia* is almost immune to all diseases and pests.

IV. *Tetraploidy*

is of interest in table grape production as the chief benefit from tetraploidy would be increase in berry size and reduction in bushiness of the vine (fewer shoots). Autotetraphoidy are found to be considerably sterile and are less productive than the parents. Allotetraploids, however, have been more desirable as commercial varieties. Examples are production of tetraploid Niabell and Early Niabell from cross between tetraploid Niagara and tetraploid campbell Early.

V. *Induction of Mutations*

Irradiation with gamma and X rays have been used to induce mutations in grapes. The most significant achievement is the production of "loss clustered" variety of perlette by irradiating the dormant cuttings with X ray at 2500 r.

VI. *Biotechnology*

Embryo rescue technique: Now two seedless (stenospermocarpic) parents can be crossed and with the aid of embryo rescue technique *in vitro,* there is possibility of getting a high proportion of seedless progeny for selection. Also, there is a possibility of increasing the number of hybrids from *vinifera x rotundifolia* crosses.

Hybdridization Techniques

(1) *Floral Biology:* Knowledge of floral biology is very essential for carrying out successful hybridization work. In grapes, the peak of anthesis and dehiscenc is between 8 and 9 A.M. and the dehiscence of pollen generally takes place immediately after anthesis. The stigmas are receptive one day before to one day after anthesis. So, the clusters of male and female parents to be used in crosses should be bagged 3-4 days before anthesis. A clothe cage should be constructed around the vines, particularly around the female parent, to prevent contamination caused by wind. The emasculation with forceps cleared regularly with 70% ethyl alcohol should be done a day or two before anthesis and then clusters bagged immediately. Pollen from the clusters of male parent should be collected between 8 and 10 A.M. by shaking the clusters against the bottom of a petri dish. Controlled cross-pollination should be done 1 day before to 1 day after anthesis with a camel hair brush used for transferring pollen.

(2) *Choice of Parents:* This is most important aspect in perennial crop breeding.

(a) *Use of female (male-sterile) vines:* Certain varieties like Pandhari Sahebi and Angur Kalan have female flowers characterised by reflexed stamens containing pollen without germpores. As mentioned earlier, these pollen do not germiante and sterility is complete. Such varieties with desirable characters should be used as female parents. In such cases, the tedious em asculation by forceps is not necessary.

(b) *Varieties with low seed viability as male parents:* They viability of seeds is largely a characteristic expressed by maternal parent. If varieties with low seed viability are needed as parents, they should be used as male (pollen) rather than seed parent.

(c) *Seedless varieties as male parents:* Seedless varieties should always be used as male parents for producing vigorous, high yielding and disease resistant new varieties.

(3) *Seed Germination and Transplanting*

Grape seeds should be ripened for about 3 months at 40-45°F to break the rest period. The stratified seeds should be sown in seed pans containing well-sterilized soil mixture to avoid damping off of the seedlings. When the seedlings are 3-4″ high, they should be transplanted to 5-9″ pots.

(4) *Field Planting*

When the transplanted seedlings are about 12″ high, they can be planted in the field in rows. When tranplanting growing seedlings all the leaves may be stripped off by hand. Normally, 5 feet distance is kept between the rows and between the seedlings. If any machine be run, the distance between the rows is increased.

The seedlings are permitted to grow without training in the first season. They are then cut back in the season and the most vigorous shoot is trained up the stake to a height of 4-5 feet then pinched back to form a head. Once the shoot is vigorous enough, fruit can be forced at any time by pruning back to a prim primary eye before it enters the rest period. However, fruit production should only be encouraged in the season considered best in the locality.

(5) *Evaluation of hybrid seedlings*

The breeder has to be ruthless in rejecting the bad seedlings. Data on each seedling to be collected for 2-3 seasons on quality & yield potential. Promising hybrids should be selected. Normally, there is one promising hybrid out of 1000 seedlings.

(6) *Testing of Promising hybrids*

Promising hybirds are given numbers and then they are tested in comparison to existing commercial varieties (standards) by adopting proper statistical design for yield, quality and other characteristics. The best ones should be tested at different centres in the country under the All India Coordinated Fruit Improvement Project and also at farmers' field. Testing can also be done at different centres within a state.

(7) *Release of variety*

Based on three years performance data, the best hybrids are released for commercial cultivation through State Variety Release Committee/Central Variety Releases Committee.

(Courtsey Dr. S.S. Negi Ex. Director CIHNP L:ucknow)

Annnexure-I
SOIL ANALYSIS REPORT

Soil Type				Clay, Clay loam, Silt loam, Silt clay loam, Sandy loam
Parameter	Unit	Value	Normal Range	Remark
pH	-	-	4.00-5.00	Acidic, use of lime is necessary
			5.00-6.00	Acidic
			6.00-7.00	Optimum
			7.00-8.00	Alkaline
			8.00-8.60 > 8.60	Very alkaline saline
$CaCO_3$	%		Less than 1.00	Optimum
			1.00-2.00	Sufficient
			3.00-8.00	High
			8.00-15.00	Reduce availability of P, Zn
			More than 15.00	Reduce availability of P, Fe, Zn, Mn
Organic carbon			Less than 0.50	Deficient
			0.50-1.00	Low
			1.0-2.00	Sufficient
			More than 2.00	High
EC	dsm^{-1}		<1.00	optimum
			1-2.0	Harmful
			2.0-4.0	Root stock needed
			more than 4.0	Not suitable for grape

Parameter	Unit	Value	Normal Range	Remark
Nitrogen	ppm		Less than 160	Low
			160-320	Sufficient
			320-480	High
			More than 480	Very high
Phosphorus	ppm		Less than 10	Deficient
			10-50	Low
			50-100	Sufficient
			More than 100	High
Potassium	ppm		Less than 180	Low
			180-500	Sufficient
			500-800	High
			More than 100	Very high
Calcium	ppm		Less than 500	Low
			500-1000	Sufficient
			More than 1000	High
Magnesium	ppm		Less than 250	Low
			250-500	Sufficient
			More than 500	High
Sulphur	ppm		Less than 10	Low
			10-50	Sufficient
			50-100	High

Parameter	Unit	Value	Normal Range	Remark
			More than 100	Very high
Iron	ppm		Less than 2.50	Low
			2.50-5.00	Sufficient
			More than 5.00	High
			More than 25.00	Very high
Magnesium	ppm		Less than 2.00	Low
			2.50-5.00	Sufficient
			More than 5.00	High
			More than 50.00	Very high
Zinc	ppm		Less than 1.00	Deficient
			1.00-5.00	Sufficient
			More than 5.00	High
			More than 20.00	Very high
Copper	ppm		Less than 0.20	Low
			0.20-0.50	Sufficient
			More than 0.50	More than required
			More than 10.00	Very high
Sodium	ppm			Optimum harmful

Annexure-II
WATER EVAULATION REPORT

Parameter	Unit	Value	Normal Range	Evaluation/rank
pH			6.00-7.00	Safe
			7.00-8.00	Manageable
			>8.00	Alkaline
Electrical conductivity	dSm^{-1}		<1.00	Safe
			1.00-2.00	Problematic
			>2.00	Root stock necessary
			>3.80	Tolerance limit of Bangalore Dogridge
			>6.00	Yield reduction of 10 % even after use of Bangalore Dogridge, yield reduction by 25 % even after use of Bangalore Dogridge
Chloride	mel^{-1}		3.0 3.00	Safe
			3.0 to 4.00	Tolerance limit of grape variety on its

Parameter	Unit	Value	Normal Range	Evaluation/rank
			>4.00	Use of own roots
			18-20	Rootstock necessary tolerance limit
			21-24	Dogridge as rootstock, yield reduction by 10 %
			26-28	Even after use of Bangalore Dogridge, yield reduction by 25 % even after use of Bangalore Dogridge
Nitrate-N	ppm		<10	Safe
			>10	Harmful-unsafe for drinking but useful for irrigation
Carbonate	Mel^{-1}			
Bi-Carbonate	Mel^{-1}			
Calcium	Mel^{-1}			
Magnesium	Mel^{-1}			
Sodium	Mel^{-1}			Low & safe High and unsafe
Potassium	Mel^{-1}		-	-
SAR	Mel^{-1}		<10	Low and safe
			>10	High and unsafe

Annexure-III
PETIOLE ANALYSIS REPORT
(October pruning)

Parameter	Unit	Value	Normal range	Remark
Nitrogen	%		Less than 0.87	Deficiency of nitrogen
			0.87-1.31 1.32-2.21	Hidden hunger, not sufficient for growths and production
			2.22-2.66 >2.66	More than required for growth development of bunches very high for growth development of bunches, growth will be fast.
NO_3-N	ppm		less than 105	Deficiency of nitrogen
			105-400	Hidden hunger, need for more N containing fertilizers and manure.
			400-747	Sufficient/optimum
			748-1168	More than required
			1200-2400	High
			More than 2400	Very high
Phosphorus	%		Less than 0.19	Deficiency of phosphorus
			0.020-0.37	Low status, not enough for growth and of bunches
			0.38-0.75	Sufficient, apply recommended manure fertilizer

Parameter	Unit	Value	Normal range	Remark
			0.76-0.95	High, for higher production P level is useful
			More than 1.00	Very high, apply P as per recommended.
Potassium	%		Less than 0.60	Deficiency of potassium
			0.60-1.13	Hidden hunger, need for more nitrogen fertilizers and manure.
			1.11-2.20	Sufficient use as per recommended
			2.21-2.73	More than required, still use of K fertilizers is necessary
			More than 3.00	Very high, use limited quantity of K
Calcium			Less than 0.53	Deficiency of calcium
			0.54-0.73	Hidden hunger, use super phosphate and foliar spray of calcium containing compounds
			0.74-1.14	sufficient containing compound
			1.15-1.35	More than required. If Ca deficiency is noticed use foliar spray or dipping of calcium containing compound
			More than 1.50	Very high

Parameter	Unit	Value	Normal range	Remark
Magnesiu m	%		Less than 0.30	Deficiency of magnesium
			0.31-0.49	Hidden hunger, need to use Mg.
			0.50-0.80	Sufficient status, use mg as per recommendations
			0.81-1.00	More than required
			More than 1.00	Very high
Sulphur	%		Less than 0.07	Deficiency of sulphur
			0.07-0.13	Hidden hunger, use sulphate of potash
			0.14-0.27	Sufficient/optimum
			0.28-0.34	More than required
			More than 0.40	Very high
Iron	ppm		Less than 10	Deficiency of iron
			10-29	Hidden hunger, use of Fe compound needed
			30-80	Sufficient
			81-200	More than required
			More than 200	Very high
Fe^{++} Iron	ppm		Less than 10	Deficiency of ferrous
			10-25	Hidden hunger, need for Fe
			More than 25	Sufficient
Manganes e	ppm		Less than 26	Deficiency of manganese

Parameter	Unit	Value	Normal Range	Remark
			26-75	Hidden hunger, need for use of Mn containing compound
			76-174	Sufficient
			175-223	More than required
			More than 300	Very high
Zinc	ppm		Less than 13	Deficiency of zinc
			13-52	Hidden hunger, need for use of Zn
			53-132	Sufficient, need for foliar spray of zinc sulphate
			More than 200	Very high
Copper	ppm		Less than 2.0	Deficiency of copper
			2.0-4.9	Hidden hunger, however, there is no need to apply Cu
			5.0-10.0	Sufficient
			10.0-100.00	More than required
			More than 100	Very high
Sodium	%			
Water soluble K	%		Less than 0.60	Deficiency of potassium
			0.60-1.13	Hidden hunger, need for more N containing fertilizers and manure
			1.14-2.20	Sufficient use as per recommended
			2.21-2.73	More than required, Still use of K fertilizers is necessary
			More than 3.00	Very high, use limited quantity of K

List of Chemicals Required for Compulsory Testing for Export

(Mg/Kg)

Sl. No.	Chemical	European Union	UK	Dutch
	Organo Chlorine Chemical			
1	Aldrin	Banned	0.05	0.05
2	Chlordane	Banned	0.02	0.02
3	Chloro thalonil	1.00	1.00	1.00
4	DDT	Banned	0.05	0.05
5	Dichloflunid	10.00	15.00	10.00
6	Dicofol	2.00	2.00	2.00
7	Dildrin	Banned	0.05	0.05
8	Endosulfan	0.50	0.50	0.50
9	Endrine	0.01	0.01	0.01
10	Lindane	0.50	0.01	0.50
11	SCH	#	#	0.01
12	Heptachlore	0.01	0.01	0.01
	Organophosphorus			
13	Accephate	0.02	0.02	0.02
14	Ageenphos methyl	1.0	2.0	1.00
15	Chloroenivphos	0.05	0.05	0.05
16	Chlorpyriphos	0.50	0.30	0.50
17	Chlorophyriphosmet hyl	0.20	0.20	0.20

Sl. No.	Chemical	European Union	UK	Dutch
18	Diazinon	0.02	0.02	0.02
19	Dichlorovos	0.10	01.10	0.10
20	Dimethoate	1.0	0.02	0.02
21	Ethion	0.50	0.50	0.50
22	Etrimphos	#	#	0.05
23	Fenchlorophos	0.01	0.01	0.01
24	Fenitrothion	0.50	0.50	0.50
25	Malathion	0.50	0.50	0.50
26	Profenophos	0.50	0.50	0.50
27	2-Chlorophenol	-	-	-
28	Methamidaphos	0.01	0.01	0.01
29	Methedethion	0.50	0.50	0.50
30	Mevinphos	0.10	0.10	0.10
31	Parathionethyl	Banned	#	0.05
32	Phoshomidon	0.15	#	0.15
33	Fosmite	Banned	#	0.05
34	Parathion methyl	0.20	0.20	0.20
35	Quinolphos	0.05	0.05	0.05
36	Triazophos Cynthate parathroid	0.02	0.02	0.02
37	Gyelothrin	0.30	0.30	0.30
38	Cyhalothrin lamda	Banned	#	0.02
39	Cypermethrin	0.50	0.50	0.50
40	Deltamethrin	0.10	0.10	0.10

Sl. No.	Chemical	European Union	UK	Dutch
41	Fenvalarate	0.02	0.02	0.02
42	Parmithrin	1.00	0.05	1.00
	Trizins			
43	Altrazin Asayalannins	0.10	0.10	0.10
44	Banlexil	0.20	0.20	0.20
45	Metalaxil	2.0	2.0	2.0
	Carbamate			
46	Carbofuron	0.10	0.10	0.10
47	Methomyl	0.05	0.05	0.05
	Paramidins			
58	Fenarimal	0.05	0.05	0.05
	Trizols			
59	Bitertenol	0.05	0.05	0.05
60	Fusiloczol	Banned	Banned	Banned
61	Hexaconozol	0.02	0.10	0.10
62	Propeconizol	0.50	0.50	0.50
	Imidozoles			
63	Imizalil	0.02	0.02	0.02
64	Captofol	0.02	0.02	0.02
65	Captan	3.00	3.00	3.00
	Dicorboxy mides			
66	Imrodine	10.00	10.00	10.00
67	Prosamidon	5.0	5.0	5.0

Sl. No.	Chemical	European Union	UK	Dutch
68	Vinchlozolin	5.0	5.0	5.0
	Benzimizol			
69	Carbandizim	2.0	2.0	2.0
70	Thiophenate methyl	1.0	2.0	2.0
	Thiocarbamate Fungicide			
71	Mancozeb	0.01	2.00	2.00
72	Maneb	2.00	2.00	2.00
73	Thiram	0.01	#	3.00
74	Propinab	0.01	#	0.02
75	Ethylene Thiourea	0.01	#	0.02
	Others			
76	Thiomethaxam	@#	@#	@#
	Oxydematon methyl	0.02	0.02	0.02
77	Fostylal	#	-	0.20
78	Copper oxychloride	2.00	20.00	20.00
79	Tridemefon	-	2.00	2.00
	Penaconozol	#	2.00	2.00
80	Sulphur	50.00	#	50.00
81	Microbutanil	1.00	#	1.00
	Denocap	#	#	0.05
	Cymaczonil	0.01	3	0.05
	Carbaryl	3.00	3.00	3.00

As per Netherland MRL can be used @ #syngenta Co. MRL 0.1 mg/kg , but further reduced to 002 mg/kg

[Courtsey Dept. of Horticulture, Mahrashtra state Pune-411005].

REFERENCES

(1) Adsule, P.G. and Anuradha Upadhaya. Grape Cultivation on root stock, National Research Centre, Pune.

(2) Adsule, P.G., Karibassapa, G.S., Banerjee, K. and Mundankar. Status and prospectus of raisin industry in India. National Research Centre for grapes, Pune.

(3) Bhujabal, B.G., Draksha Virut, Contnental publications, Pune.

(4) Chadha, K.L., and Shikhamani, S.D. The Grape, Malhotra publication. New Delhi.

(5) Shanmngavelu, K.G., Viticulture in India. Agro Botanical Publishers, Bikaner.

(6) Shikhamani, S.D. & Satish. Grape on root stock, NRC, grape, Pune.

Index

Colour Plates

Thompson Seedless

Sonaka Seedless

Sharad Seedless

Flame Seedless

Red globe

Superior Seedless.

Fruit bearing on Y - Trellis

Drip irrigation with diffusor

Diffuser (Drip irrigation system)

Covering with paper to avoid sun burn

Training System Y - Trellis

Mealy Bug
Courtsey - N.D. Sunita

Flea beetle damage
Courtsey - Dr. N.D. Sunita

Flea beetle damage
Courtsey - Dr. N.D. Sunita

Thrips damage on berries
Courtsey - N.D. Sunita

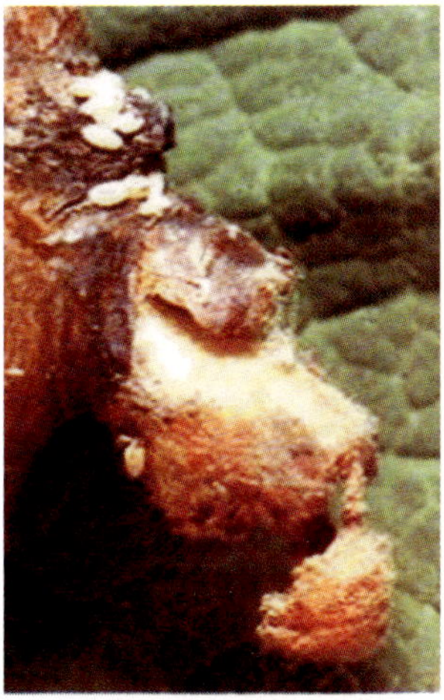

Mealy Bug on Stem
Courtsey - N.D. Sunita

Mealy Bug on Stem
Courtsey - N.D. Sunita

Sooty mould on leaf due to mealy bug
Courtsey - N.D. Sunita

Stem Borer Excreta
Courtsey -
Dr. S.B. Jagginavar

Mealy Bug in Bunch
Courtsey -
N.D. Sunita

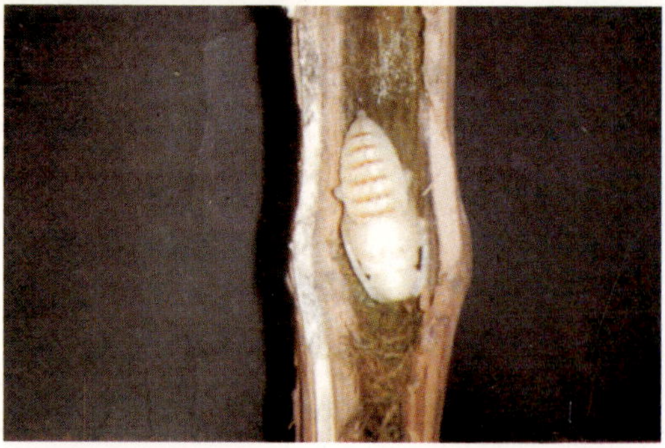

Stem Borer Pupae
Courtsey -
Dr. S.B. Jagginavar

Stem Grinder
Courtsey -
Dr. S.B. Jagginavar

Stem Borer Larvae
Courtsey -
Dr. S.B. Jagginavar

Thrips
Courtsey - N.D. Sunita

Downy mildew

Powdery
mildew

Powdry mildew

Downy mildew

Anthracnose spots on leaves and shoots of Thompson Seedless

Grape drying

Export grape box

Raisin grading

Grading Machine

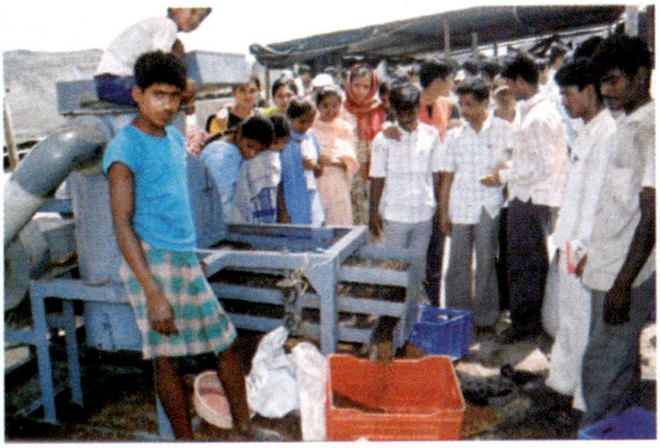

Grading Machine

Raisin in cold storage

Raisin Shed

Pre-cooling chamber

Refrigerated Van

Cold Storage

Palletization of grape

Pouch in box

Export grape packing

Grape in pouch

Stem Browning

Blemish

Excessive Sun Browning

Wind Rub-stems & Berries

Shrivelling

Powdery Mildew

Spray Damage

Surface Contamination

Circular Cracking

Splitting

80% Cap-Fall

100% Cap-Fall

Fruit Set

4 mm Berry size

6-8 mm Berry size

Girdling Stage

Bunch Closure

Woolly Bud

Bud Emergence

Three Leaf Stage

Bunch Emergence

Seven Leaf Stage

Pre-bloom Stage

Flowering Initiation

Cabernet Saluvignon

Pinot Noir

Merlot

Shiraz

Cabernet Frank

Zinfendal

Sinsat

Pinnot Blanc

Saminal Blanc

Chenin Blanc

Sauvignon Blanc

Chardonnay

Courtesy : Champagne Vineyards Ltd. Mumbai Publication Wine grape varieties, Clones & root stock compendium 2006.